IT'S A MOOD

IT'S A MOOD

Your home. Your vibe.

Cara Woodhouse

WITH WORDS AND PRODUCTION BY HEATHER SUMMERVILLE
ADDITIONAL WORDS AND STYLING BY CARA GIBBS

ABRAMS, NEW YORK

PAGE 1
A cascading light by Ronan and
Erwan Bouroullec punctuates an
architectural stairwell in Paris. Interior
design by Corinne Sachot and Gabriel
Kowalski.

PREVIOUS PAGE
A wavy, psychedelic vision in black and
white by the team at Bettencourt Manor
in Toronto.

RIGHT
A playful exploration of form designed
by Mathieu Lehanneur for the AD
Intérieurs exhibition in Paris, 2018.

Editor: Laura Dozier
Designer: Jennifer Wagner
Design Manager: Jenice Kim
Managing Editor: Annalea Manalili
Production Manager: Larry Pekarek

Library of Congress Control Number: 2024933703

ISBN: 978-1-4197-7143-9
eISBN: 979-8-88707-489-4

Text copyright © 2025 Cara Woodhouse
Photography credits appear on page 283

Cover © 2025 Abrams

Printed and bound in China
10 9 8 7 6 5 4 3 2 1

Abrams books are available at special discounts when purchased
in quantity for premiums and promotions as well as fundraising
or educational use. Special editions can also be created to
specification. For details, contact specialsales@abramsbooks.com
or the address below.

Abrams® is a registered trademark of Harry N. Abrams, Inc.

ABRAMS The Art of Books
195 Broadway, New York, NY 10007
abramsbooks.com

FOR DEAN, CASH, AND LENNON,
MY HAPPIEST MOOD MAKERS

I am obsessed with the super-saturated, wonderfully art-filled Central Hotel in Queenstown, New Zealand, where nothing is small and nothing is done to scale. Interior design by Undercurrent Studio.

The entryway to my home in Long Island is protected by two negativity-deflecting amethysts.

FOREWORD
HENRY HOLLAND

Design is a way of connecting to your innermost feelings and sharing them with the world. Whether for fashion or interiors, the choices we make when creating looks for ourselves or our homes are a way of inviting people to see *us* — the true us, the person we want the world to know.

As with fashion, creating spaces requires more than a visual connection. Good design is deeply emotional and makes for a sensory experience that is remembered long after you have left a room or taken off a gown. Our happiest memories are often informed by the environment around us — the textures, the scents, and the colors become triggers for the moods and feelings we experience in a space.

One of my biggest motivations when designing anything is the superpower it gives me to be able to affect people's mood. Creating pieces and spaces that enrich their lives, make them feel empowered, happier, and content.

Designing one's home is about creating an intimacy between the space itself and the people who are invited in. There is something deeply personal about sharing that internal part of yourself. Creating a sanctuary not just for you and your family but for all who are important enough to be welcomed in, metaphorically and physically.

Cara is a maverick in her approach to design, a warm and affectionate energy in any room. In a world that often encourages exclusivity, her ability to care deeply breaks through and, in turn, creates unforgettable and welcoming spaces, moods we all should demand from our environment.

I met Cara through friends in London, where we were always connecting at gatherings. For me, these are moments of comfort and joy — often meals shared with our chosen family. She is fascinated by everyone, making you feel seen and heard even in the noisiest of rooms. It's this innate skill that makes her such a successful designer. Creating deep connections to her clients, tapping into a profound understanding for who they are and how she wants them to feel, in a way that seems so effortless. It is what I channel myself with every bit of my creative output.

To design a space that is wholly felt is something very few people have the power to do. It is an innate skill that requires a deep understanding of one's sense of self. Cara channels this confidence so effortlessly in her work. I'm excited for the reader to see and experience this unique process. This book is an exceptional tool that teaches all of us how to dream up and make real our most personal design pursuits.

11

The Vitra Campus in Weil am Rhein, Germany, is known for its cutting-edge collaborations with (and support of) designers who skirt the norms and break all the molds. In 2024, VitraHaus invited Dutch designer Sabine Marcelis to bring to life a series of color-blocked living spaces that mix her tonal creations with Vitra's own classics. This rosy-pink bathroom, with its solid onyx tub, is simply incredible.

INTRODUCTION

Our most memorable places are not simply seen; they're felt . . . deeply.

Take a moment. Think about your favorite room in the world. Now consider why you're so drawn to it. Is it simply pretty to look at? Probably not. The more likely answer is that it makes you *feel* something, it engages your senses . . . it sets a mood. These spaces burrow in, remind us of where we've been or where we want to go, which, I will argue, is the great divide between a room that's simply well-designed and one you'll remember forever.

But how do you achieve that deeper experience through design?

This is the question I've asked myself for nearly thirty years, and the one I set out to answer in this book. After working with hundreds of clients, designing twice as many spaces, I have come to believe the answer is . . . connection. Designing from a place *of* connection—connecting to your home, to living your best life, to feeling good in your space.

Creating from this point of view becomes a deeply personal process. It's not simply about picking a chair because you need a chair or finding wallpaper because you want wallpaper. It's about looking inside and knowing what makes you happiest, then making design choices that connect you to those pursuits.

There is an undeniable link between our spaces and our mood. Even the scientific world has taken note of this overlap. Neuroaesthetics, a field of psychology that's been around since the late nineties, analyzes how our brain reacts when we experience art or listen to music. In recent years, these same psychologists have started mapping how we *feel* when we're in a particular space or setting as an extension of that.

I've always known and felt this symbiotic relationship to be true. Joy can be found in an organized kitchen drawer, good vibes in a bathroom that embraces nature, inspiration in an art-filled nook. These personal connections to our spaces make us feel lighter, happier. If you sit me at a tiny desk in a windowless room, my ability to be productive bottoms out. In this book, I explore rooms that go beyond the visual — how touch, scent, sound, and an idea I call "spirit," come together *with* sight to create spaces that are pure magic, spaces that capture a mood. Did you know there is a link between chartreuse and feeling energetic, for instance? That a piece of carnelian in a room enhances motivation? Or that the smell of coriander can ignite passion?

I consider it my job, as an interior designer, to facilitate these personal connections, to help clients define their design spirit and translate it into a sensory experience — into something beautiful that isn't simply surface deep. It would be so easy to create through the lens of a social media–dictated algorithm, or to simply cultivate my own "look" and put it on repeat. There are even designers out there who claim to know the exact formula for creating happiness in *your* home (white walls, statement chair, add a vintage light fixture and a smile). But why would you want that? Your spaces should tell the story of you. They should look, feel, and work for *you* — and no one else.

This book is a celebration of what happens when design is personal, when you create a space that is perfectly in tune with the way you live in it — when home is your favorite place in the whole world.

OPPOSITE
A gorgeous set of Raphaël Raffel chairs, designed for Maison Honoré in the seventies and meticulously restored in an ivory Belgian bouclé.

WHAT'S YOUR VIBE?

Each of the chapters in this section explores a different mood — the colors, the textures, the materials, the interesting details, how it all comes together. You may feel a strong connection to one, but it's far more likely your "design spirit" is drawn to bits and pieces of many of them. So approach each chapter with an open mind; you might find elements you love in unexpected places. And that's the point! There is no wrong answer, no box you have to squeeze yourself into. Just as we have our mood swings, so can the rooms of your home.

Mathieu Lehanneur's Familyscape Sofa upholstered in rainbow fabric by Gabriela Noelle González for Colette founder Sarah Andelman's home in Paris.

SHAKE
IT UP

For those who revel in the unexpected. Tactile experiences.
Thought-provoking combinations. Exaggerated details.

PREVIOUS PAGE

EYE CANDY ALERT
The Larose Guyon light fixture above my dining table has the sort of wow factor that defines a room. It also happens to mimic the shape of a *W*, for *Woodhouse*. Here's to happy coincidences.

ABOVE
A room that takes itself too seriously is a room no one wants to spend time in. There are two little monkeys in suits and a banana peel on the rug in our dining room for no other reason than it makes my family and me laugh.

OPPOSITE
These posters are a collection of prints by one of my favorite British artists, David Shrigley. Art does not have to be the most expensive thing in the room – in this case, it's just one of the funniest.

Could I sit here and tell you exactly what to do, exactly what to buy to transport the dining room you saw on the previous pages — which happens to be mine — to your own home? Sure. But I won't. Because if you're the type of person who wants a Shake It Up room, then you would hate that. Your inner rebel would shift into flight mode at the mere mention of "the rules." And being *told* what to do has never been a successful motivator for you. (Just ask your mom, right?)

It's that spirit, the I-create-my-own-path mindset, that gets at the heart of this approach to design. It takes nothing for granted. It wants you to ask questions, to look at things upside down and backwards, until you find your own just-right way and just-right mix. It means following your gut, not your Instagram feed.

It also, however, means practicing an almost Gwyneth Paltrow–esque level of restraint. This is not the place for more-is-more-is-more (though, if that's your speed, jump to page 120 and check out my chapter called Creative Flow). Instead, Shake It Up is about implementing a few impactful, hyper-focused moments and letting those moments sing.

Here's what I mean by that: Look carefully at my dining room. The walls and floors are a muted, light tone.

The layout is clean and simple. I don't even have crown molding in this space. That's because I wanted your attention to go to three places: the dining room table, the custom rug, and the painting on the wall — a directive that's easy to outline, tougher to pull off.

That's because when you put all your design moxie, so to speak, into three moments, those three moments have to sing. (That's a lot of pressure for a dining room table.) But here's where the push-and-pull between creativity and restraint comes into play: The flash of pattern on the panda marble tabletop is as attention-grabbing as a graphic wallpaper, but cool and unexpected coming from a table. I designed this rug to cut through the room in a winding path instead of simply skimming its edges. This keeps the long, rectangular space from feeling completely boxed in. And the painting on the wall, a commissioned piece by Brooklyn-based artist Theo Pinto, acts as an abstract mirror of sorts, echoing the intense greenery just outside the adjacent wall of windows.

There were many times when I thought about adding — adding a sideboard, maybe more wallpaper. But my gut told me enough was enough, and I listened. Sometimes what you *don't* do is just as important as what you do, uh, do.

SWEAT THE SMALL STUFF

Table legs and cabinet pulls. When you think of "wow moments," those two elements aren't typically part of the conversation. But that's what Shake It Up begs you to do. It's what *I'm* begging you to do. Stop. Re-evaluate. Don't take anything for granted.

When you put the overlooked fixture front and center, or make a functional detail the most beautiful detail, what you're doing is giving your room a visual pause. A moment that stops people in their tracks and makes them go, "OHHH," before taking in the whole space. As these kitchens prove, those pivotal moments don't have to be over the top or even big budget breakers. They can be subtle, wallet-friendly — cheeky. In the case of my kitchen on the opposite page, it was the choice to do this motley crew of oak handles (mismatched, oversized, oddly placed) that kept the room from being too serious. They are like playful punctuations, skipping across the wall in a purposefully random way. It's fun, but still chic and beautiful and interesting.

The same can be said for this pale pink banquette in Istanbul, the only space for gathering in a small pied-à-terre designed by Merve Kahraman. The layering is genius: You've got an active woodgrain, a wall of tufted pink seating, and all that art. Had she left it at that, the result would have been beautiful. But what makes it *interesting* are those table legs. A stack of black and white that's both grounding and unforgettable. Proof that a little paint is sometimes all you need.

ABOVE
Black is a neutral. White is a neutral. Black and white together is what I call a spunky neutral. It still goes with everything, but instead of melting into the background or acting as a frame for other colors, it screams, "Hey, look at me!"

OPPOSITE
FOR THE RULE BREAKERS

Every interior design textbook will tell you matching hardware creates uniformity, and that's what you want in a wall of cabinetry. Here's what I say: Forget that. The function and location of the doors and drawers in my kitchen dictated the size and placement of the hardware. Nothing is consistent, and the result is so cool and a dream to cook in.

"I could never do that" is what most clients say when they see this bathroom configuration. Does it challenge the norms? Yes. Is it tricky to replicate? Not at all! That skirting is sold-by-the-yard PVC vinyl. The stone sink is a repurposed garden trough. And that's a medium-density fiberboard (MDF) countertop. Don't be afraid to shop outside the bathroom department for bathroom materials.

Nothing is to scale in this tiny bathroom – and that's what makes it brilliant. The pendant light is bigger than you'd expect. The mirror is narrower. The checkerboard pattern is larger. The vanity is smaller. Together, though, all those "-ers" have a just-right balance.

"Just going for it" is scary. I get it. Especially if a go-for-it moment is pricey. But here's the thing: It doesn't have to be either of those things. One unexpected detail, like this toilet paper roll holder, can change the whole vibe of a powder room all on its own.

A CASE OF THE "SHOULD-BES"

Perfectly straight. Perfectly paired. Perfectly perfect.

Could there be a more boring pursuit? Personal spaces require personal design choices — and nothing waters down a creative vision faster than getting stuck in someone else's definition of perfection.

Shaking things up means shutting down the noise, designing for yourself and how you live. Only you know what you need! Every contractor in the world will tell you a bathroom vanity should be between 34″ and 36″ high. But if, like me, you're among the vertically challenged, that's too tall. I lowered mine to 33″, so the counter is about level with my hips, because that's what felt right and comfortable — and kept water from splashing all over the floor when I washed my face.

The lesson here is this: Don't get stuck in the "should-bes." Just go for it. I'll take rough-edged marble and mismatched sinks over a traditional "his and hers" bathroom layout any day of the week. Give me wildly out-of-scale fixtures. Give me a challenging color palette. Give me personality — even if your first step in this world-of-your-own-making is a squiggly toilet paper holder. I'll help you hang it.

PLEASE TOUCH EVERYTHING

A favorite hobby of mine is watching people's reactions to a space as they enter it for the first time. Where does their eye go? Do they take two steps in and stop? Or do they come in, sit down, and get comfortable? Do they tuck their hands in their pockets? Or do they walk around touching everything? (I consider the latter to be high praise.)

It goes without saying – though I am going to say it – that a room should be welcoming. It should say, "Hey, come on in . . . touch everything." And though there are many ways to go about achieving this come-at-able vibe, for a Shake It Up room, my go-to design tool is texture.

Texture can be literal, like the way the kids' room on the opposite page has those gorgeously plush throw blankets at the ends of the beds. Or it can come across in more abstract ways, through the layering of color and pattern, like the wall of tonally blocked cabinetry on this page.

In both cases, you get the biggest, must-touch-everything results when you play at opposite ends of the spectrum, pairing the super-smooth with the overly plush, layering an intricate and busy pattern with something that's big and graphic. There's breathing room in the in-between, a moment to pause – which is so important, as I've mentioned before – and take it all in.

ABOVE
How do you create visual texture with color? By layering your shades. With layers comes depth, and it's the depth that gives you texture. These Pantone-hued storage cubes are something you could easily replicate with a trip to IKEA and a bit of paint.

OPPOSITE
This Brooklyn bedroom, designed by Marc Houston, is exactly what I mean by playing at opposite ends of the spectrum. The wallpaper (from Bien Fait) is a tightly layered intersection of stripes, while the David Shrigley posters, set against a stark white background, pop the colors without competing with the pattern.

IT'S CALLED
ART-CHITECTURE

When Brooklyn creatives Fernando Aciar and Anna Polonsky were renovating their forever home, an 1899 brownstone (seen on page 41), the couple told *Domino* magazine they "let the home guide the design," and "made decisions day-by-day." Similarly, French designer Joséphine Fossey, according to Sight Unseen, began the stunning project on the previous page, a home in Provence, not with the delineation of space but with the selection of art.

Any seasoned contractor would call these approaches backwards and likely make a dash for the door (Road Runner dust cloud in their wake). But if you really want to shake things up, shirking the norm starts at conception. It means thinking of the elements of your home — especially the architectural moments — not solely in terms of function-ality but also in terms of personality, the *you* of the space.

Take this cast-concrete fireplace, for instance. Original to the Berkeley, California, home, it was built in the 1960s by a local artist named Martin Metal. It stretches from floor to soaring ceiling and is covered in textural swirls and fossilized imprints. This is a fireplace as art.

Save the eye rolls. I don't want to hear your I'm-not-creative-enough-to-come-up-with-that speech. You are — and all the inspiration you need is probably already under your roof. How would the print on your favorite dress look as a wall mural? You're obsessed with the perforated pattern on your dining room chairs. Could that pattern become something bigger — a wooden room divider or a headboard, maybe? If there is a local artist/sculptor/millworker you've been admiring, how can you collaborate with them?

Lead with what you love and approach functionality through that lens. This will take you to a creative place, always. Bookshelf as art. Banquette cushion as art. Stair rail as art. You get my point.

PREVIOUS PAGE
Picture the living room you just saw without Parisian artist Florence Bamberger's hand-painted fresco. The mid-century furniture is impeccable. But it's those lines, an homage to French master Le Corbusier, that make this Joséphine Fossey–designed space something to envy.

OPPOSITE
Consider me the newest member of the cast cement fan club. Even if this fossilized ocean scene isn't your thing, this technique — and this material — can be used in so many ways. You could create a textured lamp or a set of cool, striped side tables.

BELOW
Your local upholsterer could likely make this texture-rich, bolstered cushion moment — in any fabric — for less than that designer throw pillow you've been eyeing.

WHAT'S YOUR VIBE?

ALEX PROBA

Alex Proba is the embodiment of why you should trust your gut. The multi-hyphenated artist's signature lineup of naive, nature-inspired shapes have appeared on everything from tabletop objects to Dalí-esque totem installations commissioned for Design Miami. "I'm all about pattern on pattern, clash on clash. There's never too much of anything," Proba explains. She designs gravity-defying furniture, texturally explosive rugs, and seriously cool interactive sculptures. And her ongoing experimentation with AI-generated art is nothing short of thought-provoking.

But my first Alex Proba love was — and remains — her colorful, oversized pool murals. Viewing her amoebic forms and brilliant colors through a watery lens is pure magic. She finished her first in 2020, a pool in the backyard of a classic 1957 Donald Wexler home in Palm Springs, and has gone on to complete four more around the States — and counting. "The pool," she told me, "is such an overlooked canvas. I love opportunities like that, and I never say no to projects that involve mediums I've never worked with before."

WHAT'S YOUR VIBE?

Alex Proba–designed pool in
Rancho Mirage, California.

COME ON, LET'S ROLE PLAY

The trees in your backyard are part of your home's architecture. You planted a sculpture in lieu of shrubbery. The vegetable garden is located on your rooftop. Up is down. Right is left. And you can't be expected to keep your Shake It Up momentum contained *inside* the four walls of your home.

But before you get too caught up in what you want to do outside, look at what you already have and be realistic about what's possible. Who doesn't want a beautiful jasmine vine climbing the walls to their front door? But will that particular species grow and thrive in that location? Maybe a cool yard sculpture that allows you to have a water-conscious landscape is the better, less-temperamental option.

If a back porch is your dream, consider how important it is that it be an uninterrupted expanse. Would building around one or two or three trees ruin the vision? Or would it evolve into something better? I'm inclined to believe the latter.

OPPOSITE
The team at Alterstudio Architecture designed this Austin home around the dozens of mature trees on the property, turning them into a part of the building plan. Following an ethical mandate from the homeowners, not a single one was felled during construction.

BELOW
I love the idea of a hyper-bright door replacing colorful landscaping in a place like Palm Springs, where thriving vegetation is not exactly feasible.

ABOVE

After seeing these incredible sliding doors at
Ulla Johnson's Manhattan showroom, I went
through a phase of wanting every surface
to be perforated. Designed by Rafael de
Cárdenas, the space has such great flow
and energy.

OPPOSITE

Fernando Aciar and Anna Polonsky found
themselves in a want versus need struggle
in their Brooklyn living room. They *wanted*
something that gave the space movement, but
they *needed* the functionality of a bookshelf.
The solution: this sculptural, serpentine shelf
that snakes across an entire wall.

THE SPACE HEALER

Large furniture. Tight spaces. Is it a definite no?

In 2017, a client came to me with what I jokingly called, "the conundrum of the very large bed." She and her husband had purchased a Victorian home in New Jersey that dated back to the early 1900s. A previous designer acquired a rattan and beechwood canopy frame for their bedroom. It had a great 1960s vibe, but it wasn't really their style — and it was huge.

As the saying goes, "the older the home, the smaller the rooms" — and that was true here. So, my challenge was: How to fit a king-sized bed in their 250-square-foot bedroom without the whole space feeling out of scale.

My client was fixated on the lack of floor space. But for me, the larger issue was ceiling height. The canopy was just under 7.5 feet tall, and the ceilings were a standard eight feet. That only left a six-inch clearance.

But I always say, the first step to solving a design challenge is embracing what you can't change. Without a major renovation, which was not something the homeowners were up for, the footprint of this space was not expanding — and that bed wasn't getting any smaller. I have always thought the best small spaces are also the coziest, so my goal became: Make this room so incredibly curl-up-in-it-able that sleeping there felt like a big hug.

I used every trick I know to make those ceilings appear higher. The curtains extend from floor-to-ceiling, wall-to-wall, which gives the illusion of height. A set of bedside tables sit low to the ground, making the ceiling feel farther away. The pattern on the wallpaper travels in a vertical direction. And, the moment you walk into the room, your eye snaps up to the incredible flush mount fixture.

Then came the texture. A rug as luxuriously soft as silk. An overstuffed duvet topped with a super-chunky woven throw. An ombré bolster just begging to be your little spoon in an epic cuddle.

In the end, the fact that this bed filled up the room was not the design faux pas my clients feared. Instead, the piece of furniture they were only iffy about turned this very tight space into a room they couldn't love more.

Want to see how it
all started? Snap
here for a look at the
before shot.

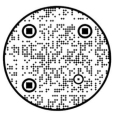

THIS IS YOUR WORLD

THE HAND FEELS . . .

Unfinished stone and texture-rich fabrics.

THE NOSE SMELLS . . .

Deep musk and sandalwood.

Citrusy linden blossoms.

A memory of clove.

THE EARS HEAR . . .

The lingering *ohm* of a singing bowl.

THE EYES SEE . . .

Active woodgrains.

Brass accents.

Checkered patterns.

Neutral walls.

THE SPIRIT CONNECTS . . .

With the twisting spires of a Euphorbia cactus.

With amethyst for calmness and wisdom.

SHAKE IT UP

THE
DARK
SIDE

Moody maximalism. Dark walls. Bright contrasts.
Quirky treasures on display.

PREVIOUS PAGE
As a general design rule, texture and saturation go hand in hand. Heavier textures, like the electric blue velvet on that amazing sofa, can make colors appear more vibrant. Dark walls amplify the effect tenfold.

ABOVE RIGHT
Homeowners Lauren Bamford and Keith Mason brought in Hearth Studio, a design practice in Melbourne, to help with the renovation of their vacation home in Tasmania. To match the charred wood exterior, they stained sheets of wood a matte, inky black that allows just a bit of woodgrain to peek through.

BELOW RIGHT
I talk a lot about objects that sing, and, well, this vibrant, geometric rug is a chromatic symphony that deserves a standing ovation. Its three sections of bold pattern help divide the multi-purpose room, separating sitting areas and directing traffic through the space.

OPPOSITE
Picture windows make up two of the four walls in Bamford and Mason's living room, meaning it's flooded with natural light for most of the day. So, if your fear of designing a dark and moody space is that it will feel like a cave, please take note.

The flickering of candles is your preferred level of lighting. Enigmatic design choices are your calling card. Sure, you're afraid of the dark, but four ink-black walls have never scared you.

That's because you're a resident of The Dark Side, a cozy refuge where the dimmers are permanently set to low. And, as happy as you are in your choice of zip code, you'd likely agree it is a place that's wildly misunderstood.

When I bring up the idea of designing a dark and moody space for a client, they often get a panicked look on their face and start talking to me about wood paneling and worn-in leather armchairs. They're looking for the fastest, politest way to shut it down. And I get that. Somewhere along the way, "dark rooms" became linked with the stereotypical vision of a gentleman's study. You know what I mean: no women allowed, lots of cigarette smoke, and brown alcohol. Dead animals hanging from the wall.

But here's the thing: Dark and moody spaces don't have to be *all* dark. They don't have to be little light-deprived lairs completely void of color. And they definitely don't have to be masculine dens. (The moody part is sort of nonnegotiable.) These dark rooms make the ideal backdrop for popping hyper-saturated color choices. Take another look at the velvety blue sofa from page 47 if you don't believe me. It's "glowing" against those stained wood walls.

Every design decision made at the weekend home you saw on the previous pages, a labor of love in Tasmania for photographer Lauren Bamford and her musician husband Keith Mason, plays on that high-drama contrast. A custom patchwork rug by local artist Esther Stewart is crisscrossed with shades of Kelly green and cobalt, crimson and lavender. The vintage Grant Featherston chaise perched by a wall of windows is covered in a vibrant shade of maroon wool. Even the little hits of white—the coffee table, the ceramic vase—seem lit from within. The design is minimal, but every detail sings.

This is not an all-or-nothing mood. There are ways to ease into it that don't even involve a single dark wall. So, please give this chapter a fair shake. Don't just look for rooms to connect with, but for moments within those rooms. The Dark Side is waiting—and, it turns out, it's a pretty welcoming place to land.

THERE'S DARKNESS IN THE DETAILS

The idea of a room enveloped in black intrigues you, but commitment has never been your strong point. Don't worry. I got you. Put down the paintbrush and back slowly away from the wallpaper. In fact, forget about your walls, ceilings, and floors altogether.

Instead, I want you to consider the elements within your space (the tables, backsplashes, even hardware) all of which can bring a vibe-y funk — no black paint required. When it comes to The Dark Side, the materials really do make the mood. Terrazzo countertops flecked in deep burgundy tones, for instance. Or a modern fireplace, like the one you see here, covered in forest green tiles.

Think about it: a big green fireplace in the center of your open living room. The potential for everything to go very wrong was high. But instead, the semi-reflective, undulating surface *is* the moment that makes this space. It subverts the mood, making it tilt more modern than rustic, despite all that wood.

The same goes for surfaces like countertops or tables. As much as I love a clean, white slab of Carrara marble, there is something so ancient and glorious about deeper shades and elaborate veining. (Flip the page to see what I mean.) These intricate stones look as though they took ten thousand years to create — and, with this mood in particular, it feels so right to have the moment that carries the room come from a material you have to unearth from the ground.

So, remember: Transitioning to The Dark Side doesn't have to mean living in a black box — all it takes is one moody player to shift the perspective.

OPPOSITE
The fact that these tiles — by Studio Kai Linke out of Germany — have a reflective finish is so important. When you have an architectural element taking up this much space, you need that bit of illusion, almost as if it's see-through, to keep the whole thing from feeling too bulky.

54

This table, a custom design by Australia's Alexander & CO, is incredible, and wow, does it set the vibe in their Bondi Junction office. The stone is called Opera d'Arte, a mix of marble, granite, onyx, travertine, and limestone pieces that have been fractured into small bits then merged back together to form a kaleidoscopic masterpiece.

FOR THE RULE BREAKERS

Retro-futuristic white oak paneling lines the walls of this incredible home designed by David/Nicolas in Amman, Jordan. The last thing you expect to find in such a light-filled space is a moody vanity moment, but it is the unanticipated contradiction — the beautiful, dark, fluted stone surrounded by all that light wood — that makes it pop.

STUDIO VISIT
GABRIEL SCOTT

SCOTT RICHLER

There is a lot of eye candy in this book, but what you need to know is that everything Scott Richler, founder and creative director of Gabriel Scott, makes is eye candy. The first time I crossed paths with one of his Welles Chandeliers, back in 2013, it stopped me in my tracks. I remember thinking, *now that's a light.*

Part of what makes Scott so impressive is his seemingly endless knowledge of lighting. It goes beyond simply understanding how to make a beautiful light fixture — though, clearly, he does. He gets how the light coming from that fixture will interact with the space it inhabits.

This is a tricky concept to master. There's a reason interior designers and architects often bring in their own lighting experts to handle that part of a project. It requires such a nuanced understanding of layering, not just in varying the types of lighting you introduce — task lighting, table lamps, chandeliers, and so on — but also the brightness of those lights. "[The right combination] is how the optimum *moody vibe* will be achieved," explains Scott.

It is from this perspective that Richler creates. "I typically work from a minute detail I have in my mind, and then zoom out to develop the full piece," he told me. Which is, by most other accounts, backwards. Typically designers start with a big picture, then get granular with the ins and outs of engineering. But instead, Richler's creations come together in curious configurations with puzzle-like joinery that evolve in order to connect the micro details of his initial vision. These movable pieces literally allow him to play with light, to control shadow, to be the master of mood . . . lighting.

JUST A LITTLE SHADOW PLAY

Funny thing about designing a dark room — it turns out your greatest tool is . . . *light*. (I know, right?) It sounds all upside-down and backwards, but the old adage about opposites attracting really does apply here. Light has a natural alchemy with dark; one plays off the other, creating a sort of shadowy magic. Out of that dance comes layers of depth — and a bit of mystery.

Take the study you see below. The incredible lacquered millwork bounces light around the small room. However, its mossy-hued surface doesn't amplify that light, like a mirror would. Instead, it emits a soft green glow. It makes the room feel both dark and moody *and* light and airy at the same time.

Painting your walls can control light in a similar way, too. Depending, of course, on the finish and treatment. (The glossier the finish, the more reflection you get.) What I love about the ombré wall in the bedroom on the facing page is that the color shifts from dark to light as your eye travels up the wall. So, the bed feels like its own cozy little cocoon down below, while the top has a floating-in-the-clouds effect.

OPPOSITE
This dramatic headboard, a custom creation by London-based interior designer Pandora Taylor, is begging to be re-created. To get those bubbling-up-the-wall moments, all you need is a round pillow and a thin piece of plywood or MDF, cut to size. Mount one to the other, then adhere the combination to the wall.

BELOW
Possibly the most unbeachy room in South Beach. I love how designers Adam Charlap Hyman and Andre Herrero of Charlap Hyman & Herrero leveled up their millwork, combining high-gloss with high-function. There's storage and a small desk hiding behind those beautiful doors.

WHAT'S YOUR VIBE?

Aged brass can occur naturally over time, of course. But it also happens if you deliberately distress the material to create a weathered patina. This treatment always feels extra-moody to me, adding an amazing layer of dimension, as you see in this primary bathroom in Brooklyn designed by Fawn Galli.

ABOVE
How gorgeous is this powder room in Manhattan, a design by Oliver Freundlich? I love the way those unexpected brass moments play off the warm tones running through the granite vanity.

THE BRASS FACTOR

The once risqué black bathroom is now considered timeless — according to every design publication around — and I am all for it. Rooms saturated in the blackest of black can be incredibly sophisticated. Especially those with a small footprint: closets, reading nooks, powder rooms. The size, the darkness . . . it's all so glamorously dramatic.

I just have one condition: If you go black, you must also go brass. Here's why: Black, similar to white, runs the risk of feeling stark and cold without the right counter-points. This metal's shiny, gold tones warm up ink-black walls. Add a few brass notes and suddenly that plain black room becomes magic. I'm not *only* talking about hardware, though. I live for a streamlined brass faucet or cool, sculptural knob. But that's a little obvious — and you can do better than obvious. Like, for instance, the full vanity done in aged brass you see on the opposite page, which is just incredible.

Look for moments to add brass that feel delicate, and others that read bold. A thin-as-thread chord from a light fixture next to a brass-blocked mirror, for instance. Having a weighty mix gives your eye multiple places to land.

So, bring on the charcoal, the jet, the onyx — even the black and white speckles of a bold terrazzo. Just don't forget the brass.

ABOVE
Part of Lindsey Adelman's crazy-cool Rock Light series, this piece of vanadinite appears as if it is being devoured by a glowing orb of light. Will the stone survive? Will it eventually be engulfed? I could watch this light forever to get an answer.

OPPOSITE
A PETA-friendly nod to the whole "men's hunting lodge" vibe, de Gournay's New York City showroom features a striking installation of their "Namban" scene, with flocks of cranes soaring across an Art Deco–inspired sky.

THE SPACE HEALER

In a house full of kids, is it possible to have a room that feels totally grown-up? The answer is yes.

Remember the height of Covid? The moment when your excitement for all that quality time together turned a corner – and you really just needed thirty minutes to yourself? Now imagine having two kids under the age of three quarantining with you. (I know some of you are going, "Check and check.") This was the case for two of my clients in Long Island.

As they watched every room in the house be taken over by their two young daughters, the realization hit that they needed to reclaim a corner for themselves. So, they reached out with an idea for a little lounge tucked beside the stairs on their main floor. They wanted moody. They wanted a space that felt as funky as they are. They *wanted* a toy-free zone. My challenge became: create an adults-only – at least most of the time – room they would want to hang out in.

Thankfully, this space can be closed off. (I'm a parent, I know closed doors don't keep kids out. But it's at least an additional barrier.) Then I considered everything needed for this room to function: A cozy landing spot, a sitting area for two, something beautiful to look at . . . a bar for mixing dirty martinis.

Initially, this was a very light and bright space. It was painted a yellow-y beige. A white wooden mantel from the nineties took up most of one wall. And old baseboard radiators lined the floor. All of which were holdovers from the previous owners. But here's the thing: The rest of the house was also very light and bright.

This room needed to be the opposite, to feel so completely different that when they entered, it felt as if they'd gotten in their car and gone somewhere else. I painted the walls and trim a charcoal gray – Deep Space by Benjamin Moore – and covered the windows in a waterfall Roman shade of the same hue. The ceiling is wallpapered in a Crescent print paper by Kelly Wearstler to fully envelope the space and achieve the intimate, lounge-y vibe they were after. We swapped the dated fireplace for an amazing custom-cut marble one. Then, we split the room in two with a very bold two-tone rug by Rug Art – bright blue for seating, bright green for the bar area (which is located opposite the fireplace).

The end result is a gathering place. One initially meant for two but, post-Covid, evolved into a spot for entertaining all their friends.

Want to see that
dated nineties
fireplace? Snap here.

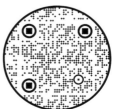

THIS IS YOUR WORLD

THE DARK SIDE

THE HAND FEELS . . .

Dense, tufted velvet and smooth, high-gloss lacquer.

The coarse finish of an exposed woodgrain.

THE NOSE SMELLS . . .

Burning embers of a palo santo stick.

A woodsy mix of papyrus and amyris.

THE EARS HEAR . . .

Flames crackling in the fireplace.

THE EYES SEE . . .

A waltz of shadows.

Reflective surfaces.

Active stone.

Saturated pops of color.

A dark backdrop enveloping it all.

THE SPIRIT CONNECTS . . .

With the inky blooms of a black hellebores.

With vanadinite clusters to boost passion, exploration, and creativity.

GOOD
VIBES
ONLY

Light and airy spaces that bring the outdoors in. Natural materials.
An earthy palette. Shoes optional.

PREVIOUS PAGE
What's so brilliant about this West Coast oasis is how the cedar-plank sauna and hot tub (you can find similar ones on Amazon) feel so naturally at home in their surroundings, like they simply grew among the succulent garden.

ABOVE
At a cliffside residence in San Francisco's Telegraph Hill, landscape architect Andrea Cochran created "gardens out of air," partitioning off tiered beds and gathering spaces, like this shaded patch for meditation that seems to float among the clouds.

OPPOSITE
When I hear "sauna," I picture a small, windowless room filled with sweaty strangers. But the view from inside this one is a wildly luxurious spin, like climbing into a telescope to take in your own backyard.

And . . . exhale.

I live for those two words at the end of a yoga class.
The moment you give yourself permission to let go
of all that heavy, holding-you-back, bad sh*t—and,
literally, breathe it all out. That single breath is like
unloading fifty pounds of mental weight some days.

But what if you didn't need to go to a yoga class to
feel that energy? You didn't need to seek out some
off-the-grid destination to get far enough away from
your life to see it clearly? What if you could feel that
lightness, find that clarity at home?

If you've been nodding and mumbling "yes, please"
through the last two paragraphs, then you're going
to want to move in and find your savasana pose in
Good Vibes Only. These rooms come at you like a
deep exhale, like the act of simply moving through
them is enough to slough off the bad juju and keep
you centered.

This mood is as much a lifestyle choice as it is a design
directive. For a good viber, well-being—physical and
mental—is priority number one. Which may sound
limiting, but if this is your world, then you know having a
hyper-focused intention is actually what keeps things
easy. A place to meditate, a spot to contemplate, a
trail for pondering—these are not optional add-ons for
you; they are a necessary part of life.

You'll see natural materials used in unexpected ways, open and airy floor plans, and so much light in these spaces. But the most important element to bringing this laid-back mood into your home is a seamless connection to nature. Blurring the lines between outside and in—and what belongs where. Plants as entryway architecture. Cement floors that flow straight into grassy lawns. Entire walls that slide open to join your home with your meditation garden.

All that good-vibe energy flows from an unencumbered ability to commune with nature. Scientifically speaking, spending time outdoors has been shown to reduce stress, lower fatigue, fight depression, boost creativity—the list goes on and on. So, imagine the benefits of having a home (or even a single space in your home) dedicated to nurturing this objective.

The backyard oasis you saw on the previous pages captures this mood perfectly. From the outside, the sauna's cedar planks look like a cool, interactive sculpture. But climb inside, and you can get lost in the amazing California landscape while unloading a day's worth of stress. Talk about a magical spot to find your exhale.

There's an ease to living this way—a perspective shift, a righting of priorities, a reckoning with what you really *need* to be happy. So, go ahead and plant a garden in your living room and move your favorite sofa to the porch, because four walls and a roof may be the accepted definition of a house, but your home is wherever the good vibes are flowing.

SHOWER MATES

I love an outdoor shower. There's something so invigo-rating about it, like the combination of fresh air and warm sunshine and being totally naked is the secret formula for clear-headedness. (Or maybe it's just the adrenaline?) But as much as I'm into the idea in theory, I am what you would call a fair-weather fan. Once the temperature dips below seventy degrees, the experience doesn't hold the same allure for me.

Which might explain why I'm so into this very groovy shower. Despite having fierce jungle vibes, it is located in a petite apartment just outside Sydney. SJB, a multi-disciplinary design/architecture firm in Australia, captured the spirit of bathing outdoors with the added bonus of, well, not having to actually *bathe outdoors* in winter. That huge, round skylight lets in so much sunshine, which, aside from being a very cool architec-tural statement, is what makes it possible for a garden of towering monstera plants to thrive in this little alcove. Even the walls are in on the illusion; this curving combination of super-active terrazzo and glossy ceramic tiles feels as if you stumbled into an opulent cave in Oaxaca.

If you only take one lesson from this glorious space, let it be this: Plants make excellent shower companions — no matter what size your bathroom. Ferns, Philodendra, and spider and snake plants do especially well in humid conditions. (Flip to page 256 to find other leafy friends that like it steamy.) Pick one or two — or ten — and never shower alone again.

OPPOSITE

FOR THE RULE BREAKERS
Who says shower handles have to be metal? These oversized, wooden, disk-shaped controls are pure magic, softening all those hard surfaces and adding another natural layer to the mix.

This 700-square-foot container home built into the hills of Belo Horizonte, Brazil, will make you reassess the necessity of proper doors. In lieu of a traditional shut-and-lock situation, interior designer Janaína Araújo surrounded the calming retreat with glass walls and perforated metal bifold doors that slide wide open for a true indoor/outdoor living experience.

The talented team at Toronto's Bettencourt Manor shared their designs-in-progress for this incredibly cool bathroom. The client requested "mesmerizing curves and raw beauty," and what they delivered — the oversized, organic forms and the hand-etched stone — is giving me chic cave woman vibes.

This is what happens when you let the landscape outside your window inspire the design taking place inside. Everything from the color scheme to the rough cedar plank walls to that amazing burl coffee table are a nod to the rolling hills of LA's Silver Lake neighborhood, where you can find artist Clare Crespo and production designer James Chinlund's living room (along with the rest of their house).

BECOMING ONE[ISH] WITH NATURE

Good Vibes Only is a plop down anywhere, dinner around the coffee table, nothing's too precious to touch way of life. But don't mistake *laid back* with *anything goes*. The mood might be low-key, but it is also elevated.

I've talked about this briefly, but I want to go a little deeper here: Nature is your best inspiration, so look outside before making decisions about what's happening inside. Take in the colors, the materials, the textures, even the organic shapes. Cultivating an indoor/outdoor lifestyle works best when there's a physical connection between the two spaces, obviously. But it also requires an aesthetic connection, a visual flow that's so in sync you don't notice whether there's a roof or open sky above your head.

Color palette plays a big role. You want it to harmonize with what's happening outside. But bringing in materials found in nature, picking soft shapes over hard lines, looking for unexpected ways to introduce stone or ceramics, are all statement moments that will really set the tone.

Take the details you see here, for instance. This gorgeous goldenrod striped fabric has a nubby woven texture, earthy palette, and twine-like tassels. The amazing vintage coffee table is encircled with agate slices. And that bench! Its undulating cushion, balanced atop three wooden balls, reminds me of an inchworm, or some other climbing creature you might find in a garden. They are all beautiful objects that began as beautiful elements of nature — and that is the spirit you want to manifest in your space.

OPPOSITE ABOVE LEFT
This vintage, seventies coffee table, by German artist Heinz Lilienthal, combines some of the most beautiful materials found in the wild — rosewood, Belgian bluestone, slate, and agate. And wow, is it a conversation starter.

OPPOSITE ABOVE RIGHT
Important lesson: Don't neglect upholstery trim! On its own, this striped Nobilis fabric has a retro slant. It's the row of tassels that flip the script, telling a much more low-key, even beachy, story.

OPPOSITE BELOW
Embracing sustainability — choosing designs that not only reflect but support our planet — is another way to bring the outdoors in. Studio Sam Klemick's Wiggle Bench is covered in deadstock canvas and has spherical orbs made of salvaged Douglas fir.

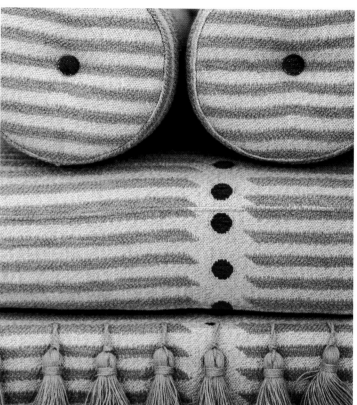

As a designer — and a human living on this planet — I feel a responsibility to encourage my clients to make sustainable, earth-friendly design choices. Which, depending on the client, is not always the easiest conversation. Cost, aesthetics, availability are all factors that come into play, and I hate to say it, but sustainability often loses out to the other, more intoxicating, lures.

But I am on a quest to educate myself and learn to ask the right questions. That's how I came across the Australian rug atelier Armadillo. They make those product debates with clients — at least when it comes to flooring — a lot easier to win. Cofounder Jodie Fried told me that from its start in 2009, "Armadillo was premised on celebrating craftsmanship, championing sustainability, and nurturing social change."

Twelve years later, they became the first Australian and American rug maker to achieve B Corp status, a standard of measuring a company's social and environmental performance. That may sound like a lengthy chunk of time, but compared to where the rest of the industry sits, is wildly impressive. And they continue to challenge themselves to be leaders in this field. All their rugs come with a Declare label, outlining exactly how it was made, what it is made of, and where it will go at the end of its lifespan. They also recently self-certified as carbon neutral.

All these credentials make it *feel* so good to buy from this brand. But I have to say, what they make — the plush piles, the woven jute, the recycled felt — is also incredibly beautiful. So, really, everyone benefits here.

One of Armadillo's most popular styles, Petra, is hand-knotted from New Zealand wool and so incredibly soft, I've had clients compare it to walking on a cloud.

OPPOSITE

The living room of artist Anne Bournas, with its awesomely random assortment of objects, proves that not every detail has to come from nature to catch these good vibes. Her concrete-based Gervasoni table, which she painted blue to match the sky, is technically an outdoor piece, while the chairs surrounding it are a mix of vintage and contemporary. There's an earthy texture coming from the ceramic lighting (by rom&an) and the braided jute rug. This nineteenth-century home in the French countryside has such spirit.

ABOVE
EYE CANDY ALERT

Vermont-based artist Karen Gayle Tinney is responsible for these stunning creations. Her work combines ceramics and fiber in a way that gives each solid vessel movement and so much personality, like it's dressed up and ready for a night out.

GO AHEAD AND SCALE IT, TIMES TEN

In the interior design world, *laid-back* and *minimalist* often go hand in hand. But I wouldn't be me if I didn't prioritize a bit of the unexpected in every room. Celebrating the ease of the great outdoors while indoors doesn't have to be minimal or restrained or anticipated. Good Vibes Only, after all, is about freedom of expression. And what could be freer and more unpredictable than the details found in the wild? The pattern of an active woodgrain. The electric hues in a coral reef. The miraculous complexity of a piece of marble, each slab unique.

I know I've talked a lot about nature and natural materials in this chapter . . . but stick with me for one more rant. Because the way to add an element of surprise to a Good Vibes Only space is to be a bit cheeky with the scale of those raw materials, taking what would typically be a small touch and making it a big moment.

Here's what I mean by that: We are all familiar with a chunky throw, but the one you see at the end of the bed on this page is extra — the yarn is *extra* thick, the knots are *extra* intricate, the weave is *extra* open. It feels almost as if the bed's been snagged by a fishing net (which is appropriate since this bedroom overlooks the dunes in Amagansett, New York). Even with all the other beautiful things in this space, your eye goes straight to that blanket.

So, if you're a bit of a statement-maker who also happens to be a nature lover who also happens to want that laid-back, Good Vibes Only life, don't be afraid to go big and bold — and have a little fun while you're at it.

OPPOSITE
The throw blanket may be stealing the glory, but don't overlook this room's other nods to the great outdoors: the live-edge wood headboard, sliced from a single tree; the puddle effect on the rug's edge; that complex neutral palette. The design, by Elena Frampton of Frampton Co, is earthy and brings the funk.

ABOVE
Son Blanc in Menorca, Spain, is an eco-retreat, opened in 2023, with the goals of being self-sufficient and having the smallest possible environmental footprint. French studio Atelier du Pont used local, natural materials as much as possible in their design, which included tapping artisans Jaume Roig and Adriana Meunié to collaborate on this untamed installation of sprouting carritx grass that hangs from its walls.

THE PLANT
PARADIGM

You're feeling these laid-back spaces, but — logistically —
you have questions. The landscape outside your front
door is nothing but cement and skyrises. Your home's
flow doesn't exactly *flow* outdoors. There aren't enough
windows in any of your rooms to even talk about a view.
Is it still possible to pull off a Good Vibes Only space?

I hear you, and there is a single answer to all these
doubts: plants. A spray of palm leaves, an arrangement of
succulents, even a full-grown tree if you have the space.
Creating a lush oasis *indoors*, cultivating a view *inside*
your walls, instead of beyond, can get you pretty close to
the indoor/outdoor mood you're after.

Here's how I know this: The sitting room you see on
these pages is mine. It has a wall of little windows and
no outdoor access, but I wanted it to feel light and open
and airy. So, I chose a palette inspired by the outdoors.
I brought in lots of wood and stone and earthy textiles.
And then I turned to a few well-placed plants — string of
pearl succulents dangling from the bookshelf, a fiddle
leaf fig tree guarding our reading nook — to really make
this room feel connected to the forest that surrounds it.

Choosing the right plants — and the right plant pairings —
is key, so for more advice on that front, jump over to The
Foliage Files on page 256, where I talk about how to
make good choices when it comes to picking green friends.

The Foliage Files on page 256

ABOVE
These custom bookshelves are
one of my favorite moments in our
home. When faced with a styling
opportunity as big as this, the thing
to remember is . . . you gotta mix it
up to make it magic. All those clean
lines needed a counterpoint, so I
added a lot of organic shapes: wild
foliage, ceramic vessels, and little
glass objects.

OPPOSITE
Our neighborhood is very "woodsy."
I decided to have a little fun with
that idea. The veins on the marble
covering our fireplace resemble
an active wood grain. And instead
of going over-the-top with plants, I
lined the underside of our benches
with birch logs.

At their vacation home in Menorca, Spain, Christophe Comoy and Luis Laplace (founders of Laplace architecture firm in Paris) used a single pane of yellow-tinted glass to create a continuous, joy-filled glow in their bathroom. Even on a cloudy day, this room is pure sunshine.

ABOVE
If this chair could talk—because it sure looks like it can—I feel like it would be singing the theme song to *Fraggle Rock* on repeat. There is so much personality packed into Ryan Belli's "Hoodoo" Chair, a reminder that when you forget to have fun with design, mood isn't the only thing that falls flat.

THE SPACE HEALER

A neglected, century-old garage begs the question: Is there such a thing as too old to save?

If it were pre-2017, you would be parking your car in this space instead of parking yourself at the gorgeous bar. That's because for around a hundred years, it was a detached garage sitting next to a turn-of-the-last-century Victorian home in New Jersey.

When my clients first brought me to see the small structure, from the outside, it looked like a risky endeavor with potential. A lot of original details and stunning moldings were still intact. Inside, it was exactly what you'd expect a very old garage to be: oil-stained floors, ramshackle storage shelves, cobwebs everywhere.

Despite everything on the interior screaming, "Tear me down," the 350-square-foot space did have one thing going for it: location. It was situated adjacent to the family's pool. So, in an attempt to redirect the wet bodies away from the main home, the ask became: Can the little garage find a second life as a pool house?

Good thing I like a challenge because this was a big one. Most of my budget went to fixing structural issues, including all new windows and a new roof, so I had to keep the space's intention hyper-focused — an area to address snack time and family gatherings — to keep my costs in check.

Two sets of glass doors keep traffic flowing smoothly between the pool, the pool house, and the main home. The wall and ceiling were covered in inexpensive shiplap, and I designed a graphic mosaic out of cement tiles for the floor — two materials purposely chosen for their ability to withstand heavy-duty use. The little kitchen is loaded up with storage. And those rope-wrapped globes, by Cuff Studio, are like twin moons when the sun goes down and the pool is still full.

We did pause for a lengthy back-and-forth about whether the room needed a big table or a long bar. Ultimately, the bar won, which ended up being a stroke of serendipity, because as my client's kids have gotten older, this little garage-turned-pool house has morphed into a highly trafficked destination for the couple's friends and neighbors.

Want to get a look
at the original garage
before I got my hands
on it? Snap here.

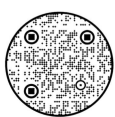

THIS IS YOUR WORLD

GOOD VIBES ONLY

THE HAND FEELS . . .

Textures made by nature.

Raw edges. Smooth ceramics.

Nubby fabrics: wools, bouclés, and corduroy.

THE NOSE SMELLS . . .

Eucalyptus.

Newly cut cedar.

Fresh air.

Wildflowers warmed by the sun.

THE EARS HEAR . . .

Rustling branches in the breeze.

THE EYES SEE . . .

Nature everywhere.

The past and present at play.

An earthy palette shot through with saturated brights.

THE SPIRIT CONNECTS . . .

With the broad leaves of a fiddle leaf fig.

With shiva lingam stones to tie us to the Earth and the ones we love.

RETRO NOSTALGIA

A nod to the past with a modern slant. Vintage-y hues.
Patterns at play. Elements of nana.

PREVIOUS PAGE
I'm just gonna say it: There's a cat on the table. The second-best thing happening in Zoë Foster Blake and Hamish Blake's kitchen in Sydney is the layered banquette seat. Leather on textured wool in a vintage, rusty shade — so good.

ABOVE
Even the mounted wall lamps in this YSG Studio–designed space have an old-meets-new clash. They are by Servomuto and feature a modern, striped fabric wrapped in old-school rattan.

OPPOSITE
In a room of so many great details, it's easy to miss what's happening under that island. The custom-designed travertine pavers on the floor flow right up the toe kick creating a very cool floating illusion.

Flipping through this chapter feels like a warm
hug from your grandma. Only she's not a *regular*
grandma . . . she's a *cool* grandma (to borrow a
joke from Amy Poehler's character in *Mean Girls*).

The same vintage-y details you would expect
are at play: checkerboard prints and plaid,
mohair and quilting, wallpaper, and lots of tile (in
the bathroom and beyond). But the scale is off,
the application is unpredictable, the shelves of
knickknacks are cooler. And there's no linoleum
on the floor. These spaces capture the spirit of
the past and plant it firmly in the now — with a
healthy sense of humor intact.

To be clear, this mood is not about buying old
things. The truth is, you'll find very few truly old
things on these pages. But the influence is there.
If this is your happy place, you know this vibe is
more about connections — to people, to memories,
to the past. Finding things that give you the warm
fuzzies and cherishing them because they do.
You've experienced a lot of places in your life,
but nowhere quite like your grandparents' house.
It had charm. It was cozy. And yes, sometimes it
smelled a little funny. But hey, that's all part of
what you loved about it.

The retro-leaning aesthetic of the eat-in kitchen
you saw on the previous pages is exactly the
vibe I'm talking about. It is located in Sydney and
belongs to Zoë Foster Blake and Hamish Blake,
and if you are at all familiar with the couple — she's
an author/beauty entrepreneur, he's a comedian/
presenter — you know their love for bygone eras,

specifically the sixties and seventies, is well-documented. (Please take a minute to search for photos of their epic, 1964-themed tenth wedding anniversary party.) "[Those decades] were wild," Foster Blake told *Vogue Australia*. "[It] is my favorite design era. Loads of pattern, unbridled color, and lots of joy."

To get the retro-modern mix just right, the couple brought in local interior designer Yasmine Ghoniem of YSG Studio, who interpreted their list of wishes — "rich and texturally exciting" and "elements of nana" — in a completely out-of-the-box way, especially when it came to material selection. In the eating nook, for instance, the rust-colored banquette and the use of rattan are both throwbacks, but the custom red lacquer table and the amazing arch surround couldn't be more of-the-moment.

That push-and-pull continues throughout the room. The stripe feels traditional, but putting it on a countertop using two contrasting types of travertine is totally modern. The wallpaper composition is straight out of your grand-mother's house, but the amplified scale makes it all a little wacky. (Foster Blake calls it "a case study in the effectiveness of wallpaper," and, well, she can consider me convinced.)

Old things that feel new. New things that look old. The timestamp is a bit hazy, but it all makes itself at home here — and I say, lean into it. Let those feel-good nostalgic vibes wash over you.

HEY, WATCH YOUR TONE

When I picture the 1970s, the one color that comes to mind is terra cotta. It's warm. It's earthy. It reminds me of that amazing scene filmed at a John Lautner house from *Diamonds Are Forever*, the one where the female villain somersaults off Gaetano Pesce's Up chair (upholstered in a terra cotta fabric) and kicks Sean Connery's ass. As a material, it is timeless. As a color, however, the saturated shade throws off strong vintage vibes that can feel a bit dated if the tone is wrong or the design plan skews too old-school.

Inverting expectations is one way I bring this shade into the twenty-first century. Here's what I mean by that: People expect a terra cotta tile, but not a terra cotta–colored marble. They expect a rough clay surface, but not a soft, cushiony seat. In other words, let the color be the throwback, and make the form unexpectedly modern.

Just as important (possibly more, actually) is the tone you choose. If you do some historical digging, you'll see that the terra cotta of the seventies has a bright, orange-y tint, while today's iterations tend to be deeper and lean more pink-ish/burnt sienna than sedated coral.

Since we're on the subject, let's talk about avocado green, mustard yellow, and lavender, too. The same concept applies to these vintage-y hues. Look for today's interpretations. Avocado green should be minty and soft. Mustard yellow . . . brighter, less muddy. And lavender is best when it's a pale, almost translucent hue. The contrast might seem miniscule, but it makes all the difference.

ABOVE
The warmth radiating from this living room in Paris, the home of fashion designer Vanessa Cocchiaro, comes almost exclusively from the inclusion of that curving terra cotta sofa, a custom creation by her architect Diego Delgado-Elias. It reads as quiet and minimal, just a well-chosen pop of color making all the difference.

OPPOSITE
See that cool stripe on the front of those drawers? It's not an inlay, but a very smart use of wood stain. The effect is so good — and so budget-friendly. Two cans of Minwax cost less than twenty bucks. Interior design by Australia's Flack Studio.

FOLLOWING PAGES
FOR THE RULE BREAKERS
Lining a living room in sheer curtains isn't necessarily groundbreaking, but when those sheers are minty green — and there's a mustard-yellow striped sectional involved — you're going to stop and pay attention. Interior designer Sally Breer created this retro den for an LA-based couple who asked that every room feel intimate and saturated.

SUPER-SIZE ME, PLEASE

Plaids and stripes. Colorful geometrics. Checkered prints. In the timeline of design history, they've all come and gone and come again, each time taking on a new persona that speaks to the cultural zeitgeist of that particular era. What I love about this family of patterns is that they tend to play well together, especially when you mix generations—a sixties' block-print with a fifties' check with a twenties' pinstripe. It all works.

In their latest embodiment, however, these throwback motifs look as if they traveled through a magnifying glass and came out the other side bigger, bolder, and hairier than ever. (More on that last one below.) The Pierre Paulin Pacha lounge chair you see opposite is a great example. The style dates back to the mid-seventies, but the Pierre Frey fabric covering it feels like a super-saturated eighties plaid, only blown up ten times larger than you'd expect. So, in the end, this very vintage mix reads cheekily modern. Even the muted striped rug is out of proportion—the lines are wider, more audacious, and of the moment.

The amplification doesn't stop at oversized prints either. There's an unchecked textural landscape happening here. The plaid fabric is a mix of virgin wool, mohair, and alpaca—each left intentionally, uh, hairy. (We're talking brushable amounts of fiber length.) It's tough to see in this photo, but the rug—the work of British fashion designer Kitty Joseph—has a dizzying height disparity between stripes, one towering over the other creating an amazing wave effect. The tufts seem to change color depending on your position in the room.

Today's patterns may be bigger and the textures wilder, but all that old-school charm remains solidly intact. Make brave choices—and don't leave your sense of humor at home.

OPPOSITE
Designers like to talk a lot about developing layers in a room, it's how we add life to a space. Texture is the most important element to get right, and this room nails it. Stone, wood, seagrass, striped wool, extra-long mohair—a little bit of everything in just the right amounts.

BELOW
EYE CANDY ALERT
Turkish architect and interior designer Irem Erekinci created this retro café concept for a client in Korea. The patterned wall makes such a statement, but it's the custom cobalt blue sculpture that's giving me some serious throwback vibes.

A LITTLE GOES A LONG WAY

If all this retro nostalgia has you feeling warm and fuzzy all over, but designing a whole room to fit the mood is a little less tempting, I get it. My advice, if you have that concern, is: Don't do it – at least not the whole space. For this aesthetic in particular, you only need one biggish moment to achieve that throwback magic. A single decorative pillow isn't going to do it. But an area rug or a cool piece of furniture, even a well-placed section of tile, is enough to try it on for size.

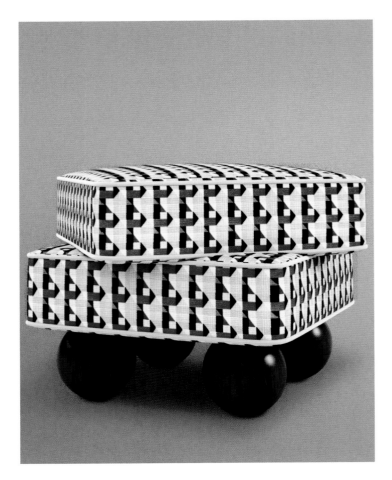

OPPOSITE LEFT
Such a hilariously literal take on "classics with a twist." I would flank a fireplace with a set of these Madonna ottomans by Malabar, a furniture maker out of Portugal, to create the most incredibly cozy moment.

OPPOSITE RIGHT
Plaid, but make it oversized. Wool, but make it texturally diverse. I can't get enough of the playful contradictions – and the serious grandpa mood – vibrating off this geometric rug by Scandinavian artist Evelina Kroon.

ABOVE
Is there ever a wrong time for checkerboard tile? These – by Sara Watson of Balineum – are such a graphic contrast to the very traditional historic mantel in a Brooklyn brownstone designed by Jesse Parris-Lamb.

ALWAYS ON THE CHARM OFFENSIVE

When it comes to vintage details in a home, one person's charm is another person's eyesore. Maybe you love a wood-paneled den, and the fact that the mid-century home you just toured has one is the greatest selling point of all? Or maybe you finally found the perfect apartment to rent, but it comes with a wallpapered bathroom that reminds you of your great-aunt Shirley's (which is not a bonus)?

Either scenario can lead to incredibly inspired design moments. If you're more a nay than a yay, don't automatically nix that perfect home or rental apartment over one dated detail. Instead, look at it as an opportunity to test the outer limits of your creativity. Some of my most-favorite design moments started with a problem that needed to be solved. Dated kitchen cabinets can be refinished. Old doors can be replaced. If there's a will, there's a way . . . to design around it.

Take this entryway for example. It's part of a 1940s modern home just outside LA, bought by Rachel Craven, a sustainable clothing designer, in 2018. It had carpeting throughout, and what seemed like acres of dark-wood paneling. The floor was an easy enough fix, as were the walls. But removing the entryway's geometric stained-glass panels would have been a pricier update — and, well, you have to pick your battles. So, they stayed and became the one colorful moment in a mostly neutral home. By keeping everything else in the entryway — including a geometric print by Craven's father — minimal and playfully modern, the stained glass felt less old-fashioned.

OPPOSITE
If, like me, you lament that your home doesn't have a glowing stained-glass moment, don't brood — make one. You can buy colored panes at almost any glass and mirror store, and the glazier will measure, fit, and install them. I love this idea for a shower enclosure!

ABOVE
My favorite way to embrace a design challenge: humor. If you can't change the yellow strawberry patch–printed wallpaper, one-up the wackiness, as my friend and fellow designer Harry Heissmann did, by adding a big, Oaxacan wood snail climbing its vines. It's a guaranteed smile-maker.

OPPOSITE

Part of the Soft Blown collection, a collaboration between Nichetto Studio and Lladró, this limited-edition table lamp is a hit of unexpected texture from a material usually prized for its glass-like smoothness.

NIEVES CONTRERAS

What I love most about Lladró is that they are not simply making beautiful porcelain objects; they are creating cherished heirlooms. It fascinates me how something so small can come to mean so much to someone, how it can embody so many memories. The Spanish brand has been around since the 1950s, but I remember back in the eighties, collecting their whimsical figurines was almost a sport, with women displaying their glass menageries as a point of pride.

Today, under Nieves Contreras's creative direction, Lladró has transformed the mere tchotchke into a work of art and upped its collectability with incredible, limited-edition artist collaborations (Jaime Hayon and Camille Walala are a few of my favorites). Despite the material being around for two thousand years, at Lladró, Contreras explained, "we consider porcelain a very modern material because it has endless possibilities in terms of shapes and colors." In other words, they're not just making dainty figurines these days.

Take their Boldblue and Boldblack collections, which utilize hyper-pigmented color to create drama, or the Soft Blown lighting collection, a collaboration with Nichetto Studio that uses balloon art as inspiration for its playful shapes. "It's all about meaning," says Nieves, "pieces that arouse good feelings." Pieces, I would add, that embody a story and create a connection that lasts generations.

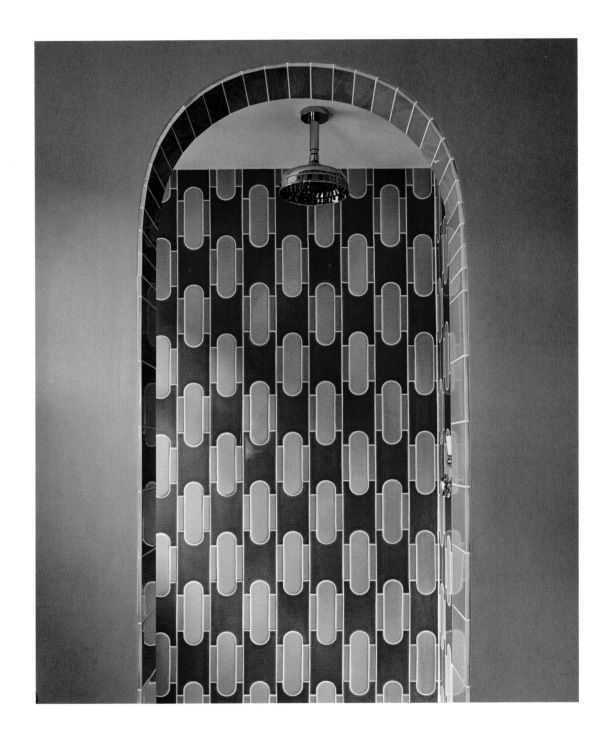

ABOVE

Plenty of people love vintage tile in a bathroom. I, however, am more into "vintage-looking." The tile in Pandora Taylor's London bathroom (a geometric design by Fornace Brioni) makes me want to have a dance party in her shower. I love that instead of countering the dated architecture with something modern, she doubled down and went bolder, more retro.

OPPOSITE

A chromatically confident mix from the ladies behind LALA Reimagined. This is a lesson in giving something an old soul without having it feel just plain old. Both the wall color (Red Earth by Farrow & Ball) and the geometric striped fabric are a nod to the past, but that beautifully odd dragonfly sconce (from Luci di Seta) recalibrates the mood to feel totally now.

THE SPACE HEALER

Run-down exterior. Limited budget. Can it be done?

My family's mid-century ranch in Long Island was built in 1961. It had one previous owner before us, who had not invested in a lot of updates over the decades. Which is to say, the exterior needed heaps of love, and my challenge was how to do that without spending a lot since I was taking on the entire home at once. Structurally, the house was sound. But nothing eats up a budget faster than windows, doors, and exterior materials — and it all looked well beyond its sell-by date.

The simplest path forward seemed to be painting the house all one color. But the answer turned out to be easier (and cheaper) than I expected. Before you can paint brick, you need to power wash it. In the middle of that undertaking, I realized our bricks were not muddy brown, just covered in decades of actual mud. Hundreds of gallons of water later, we found very cool deep taupe walls. The lesson here: Clean first, then make design decisions.

That one discovery convinced me to fully embrace the home's mid-century aesthetic. I sanded and stained the teak panels and repaired the few spots that needed it. The windows, which were plexiglass (can you believe it?), were all upgraded with modern, double-paned glass — my biggest investment by far. And we replaced the wildly overgrown shrubbery

with clean, low-to-the-ground landscaping, which balanced the flat roofline.

My last obstacle was swapping out the very weathered front door, which I always say is like shopping for glasses, because whatever you pick is going to set the tone for your whole look. The best advice I can give you is to let the style of your house — mid-century modern, in my case — dictate the style of your door. This is not the moment to go rogue. Don't be afraid of the closeout retailers either, which is where I found this one. It is mahogany, so I was able to stain it to match the teak surround. But you can always buy an inexpensive door and paint it a fun color, which was my original plan.

When all was said and done, I spent less than ten percent of my budget on this exterior upgrade — which certainly wasn't nothing, but it was a far cry from the price tag of a complete overhaul.

Want to see the
muddy brown before
shot? Snap here.

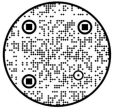

THIS IS YOUR WORLD

THE HAND FEELS . . .

Extra-long mohair and worn-in leather.

Smooth aged wood and seeded glass.

Cut piled rugs underfoot.

THE NOSE SMELLS . . .

A bouquet of roses.

Lemon and orange blossom.

Traces of Grandpa's patchouli.

THE EARS HEAR . . .

The crackle of a record as the needle drops.

THE EYES SEE . . .

An unchecked textural landscape.

Curving silhouettes, vintage-y hues, patterns gone wild.

THE SPIRIT CONNECTS . . .

With an aloe plant perched on a kitchen windowsill.

With moonstone for rebirth and renewal.

RETRO NOSTALGIA

CREATIVE
FLOW

A respite for the inspiration seeker.
Art first. Sculptural influences. Color everywhere.

PREVIOUS PAGE
Fun fact: Fluorescent yellow is my favorite color. Would I do an entire room in the electric shade? Probably not. But as an accent, a little splash of this hyper-hue has become one of my signature design moves.

ABOVE
One wall of my bedroom had to be delegated to wardrobe storage. But I really didn't want that wall to scream "I am functional!" So I added raised, oversized handles to give the built-ins dimension and a sculptural finish.

BELOW
I designed the custom rug with the team at Stark to mirror the drip on the Calico Satori wallpaper. But we decided to flip the color scheme — make the drip dark and the rest of the rug white — to keep the room feeling light and airy.

OPPOSITE
My happy place happens to be a marble slab yard. (That's why I have a whole chapter dedicated to stone — see page 148.) I especially love using it in unexpected ways, like the solid block of marble jutting off the side of my custom bedside tables I designed for my bedroom. It adds an extra layer of materiality to the space. (Plus, it's so damn cool.)

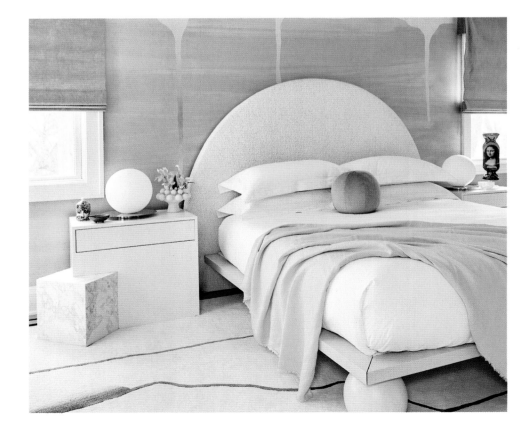

WHAT'S YOUR VIBE?

In design, as in life, you crave the creative experience, not the finished product. Your space is an ever-evolving canvas—the one place you've given yourself free rein to follow artistic whims and innovative inklings. Electric pink tile on the ceiling? For sure. Safe word? Nah, you've never needed one. Any vision worth dreaming up is worth trying out.

Sound like you? Well then, hello, my creative flowing friend. By letting your artistic spirit take the lead, your spaces are both inspired and inspiring. The brilliance you pull off with only a brush and a can of paint is trans-formative. You're not afraid to funk things up (despite occasionally f*cking them up first). But hey, that is a part of the process. Creativity is messy—it's supposed to be.

Take my bedroom, which you saw on the previous pages, for instance. My husband, Dean, and I had one goal for this space: It had to be somewhere we could turn off. With that in mind, I set out on a minimalistic journey—white walls, blackout shades, delicious bedding you could melt into. No distractions. The result was . . . totally boring. We hated it almost immediately.

We're both creatives, and to have a bedroom void of all personality turned out to be more maddening than Zen. The room you saw on the previous pages was not the result of a one-and-done design plan. It took time—lots of it—and went through a half-dozen iterations (and counting!). But we're okay with that. Because what we came to realize was that this space not only needed to be somewhere to simply turn off our minds and bodies, but it also needed to recharge our creativity.

To do that, we had to find and fill our bedroom with moments and things we could connect with and be inspired by, like the pale, icy blue color, the most calming shade imaginable. I plucked it out of the drippy, Calico Satori wallpaper you see on the walls. The custom Stark rug is shot through with matching blue veins, and the velvet window treatments make the whole space feel like you're sleeping in a cocoon.

Rounding it all out (literally) were as many curving, swooping design elements as possible, from the Entler Studio light fixture to the wooden balls our bed sits on. I wasn't about to let four walls box in my creative flow—and neither should you.

A MATTER OF PERSPECTIVE

If you have ever spent time in art school or taken an interior design course, you've likely heard a whole lot about "the trained eye," a term used to sum up the idea of teaching yourself to see the unobvious elements of a space.

I've gotten some pretty wild advice over the years on different ways to switch up your perspective. Spin around in a circle as fast as you can, then quickly pinpoint the colors that stood out. Walk into a room and immediately squint so you can take in the sight lines and nothing else. It feels sort of like a Rorschach test: One woman's bat is another woman's butterfly is another woman's inkblot wallpaper.

But there is some truth to these techniques — the idea of physically changing your interaction with a space to achieve a new perspective. Take a look at the entryway on this page. See that sliver-of-a-wall between doorways? Most people would pay no attention to it. But if you are the type of person to go with the Creative Flow, you see things a bit differently — and leaving those three-ish feet of wall barren is nothing but wasted potential. Especially when you can turn it into a wow moment like this.

The same concept applies to the very traditional wall of built-in-cabinetry on the opposite page. Painting it white and filling it with books is the obvious choice. It takes a very brave person to dream up and follow through with what you see here. Powdery blue casing and warm peach shelves are daring on their own. To shoot a floating cobalt staircase straight through the center is pure genius.

So, whatever you need to do to broaden your perspective — stand on your head while smelling a daisy? — just do it. It can't hurt, and tapping into your silly side can lead you to the most wildly creative places.

OPPOSITE
Designer Marianne Evennou had fewer than 300 square feet to work with in this Parisian apartment, so every creative decision had to pull its weight. The floating staircase leads to a tiny sleeping mezzanine and doubles as a desk.

BELOW
I'm convinced interior designer Edward Yedid is a magician. His ability to create the illusion of movement in this makeshift entryway is applaudable. The combination couldn't be more by-the-book, but the fact that everything is just a little bit off makes all the difference.

FOLLOWING PAGES
This is what I mean when I say take your time and let the magic happen. Franck Genser, the incredibly talented designer (of furniture and interiors), spent a year dreaming up a plan for his Parisian apartment and nine additional months bringing all the whimsical details, like a setting pink sun installation in the dining room, to life.

THE UN-OBVIOUS CHOICE

What I am about to tell you might seem a bit controversial but hear me out: I want you to second-guess yourself. Not all the time, and not with your most daring design choices. Those I want you to go for. But when you come at a decision instantaneously, seemingly without thought, try to get in the habit of pausing and asking yourself: "Did I actually make this choice because it feels like me, or did I pick the most obvious option?"

It's easy to get caught up in the "what's trendy" design flow. But when you do that, your own creative flow has nowhere to go. Russell Whitehead and Jordan Cluroe, the London designers behind 2LG Studio, talked about this idea with *Dezeen* magazine: "When we launched our business [in 2013] we were made very aware of boundaries and rules and the 'right' way to design . . . [but] we wanted to dive straight into the middle of that and hold firm to what we loved."

There is no color wheel in the world that would tell you to pair a vintage-y bubblegum pink with cobalt blue. Two bold shades, one small bathroom? A terrifying choice for even the most seasoned designer. But Whitehead and Cluroe held firm to their mantra, and what they created is a bathroom that radiates pure happiness. Who wouldn't want to start their day in front of that mirror?

OPPOSITE

FOR THE RULE BREAKERS
Vanity lights are notorious scene stealers. But if you could see the rest of this bathroom, you'd know there is plenty of light. Opting for understated, little porcelain fixtures (by Michael Anastassiades) to flank the mirror instead is in keeping with the designers' lead-with-what-you-love approach.

STUDIO VISIT
MATHIEU LEHANNEUR

MATHIEU LEHANNEUR

Mathieu Lehanneur creates in a space where rigid borders and set definitions don't exist — only imagination. The multidisciplinary French designer challenges all perceptions, including those put on the materials with which he works. His Inverted Gravity collection balances hundred-pound slabs of marble on blown-glass legs, replicating, he says, "a floating state where the notions of heavy and light have no more meaning." The concept came to him in a dream, the idea of reversing the "eternal typology" of a delicate glass vase, which is typically placed *atop* a sideboard. The inversion creates an unending magic trick for the mind. He also recently dreamed to life Suite N°4 (an open-air hotel room meets your cruising-around-town car) for Renault, and the 2024 Paris Olympic torch — no big deal.

He's even flipped the way we interact with the furniture we live with. His Familyscape Sofa series is beyond brilliant. As he explains it, "I like that a piece of furniture does not dictate how to sit . . . chat, sleep, debate, or reflect, feet on the ground or legs in the air." When I first saw one at his studio, it was covered in a beautiful white velvet. But then, Sarah Andelman, the founder of Colette in Paris, went and upholstered hers in a rainbow fabric by Gabriela Noelle González (see page 18) and blew my mind.

WHITE GOES HIGH-IMPACT

White isn't exactly known for bringing the drama. But I'm here to tell you, it can be a total diva.

People have equated painting a room white and approaching a blank canvas since the beginning of time. I won't argue with that analogy. But I think those same people often let all that white get the better of them. They make timid choices. They play it safe. For what? To maintain the pristine white surfaces? News flash: Those surfaces *want* to be disturbed. They want exaggerated details, striking architecture, and unexpected furniture choices. They want to be interesting.

The line between beautifully minimal and completely sterile is paper thin. Too few things are a bore. Too many become chaotic. So, if you've chosen to walk this narrow path, you must be a person who isn't afraid of big, bold design decisions. (I would actually argue that choosing to design a room in nothing but white is, in itself, a big, bold design decision.)

Then there's the battle of picking the right tone. When this book went to press, Benjamin Moore had 177 shades of white paint in its library. (Talk about intimidating!) Here's how I edit a selection like that down to find a high-drama white: Go with something bright, clean, and crisp. Skip anything with gray or yellow undertones. My tried-and-trues for rooms like these are Benjamin Moore White or Super White.

Whatever color you choose, buy a sample and try it in your space first. If I'm deciding between multiple shades, I like to order big swatches, hang them on all the walls, and live with them for a bit. It's important to see how each one interacts with the light at every point in a room, at every time of day. Once I've whittled down the options, I go back, paint a large sample (again on each wall), and repeat the final step above. There's nothing more frustrating than painting a whole room, only to later decide the color is all wrong. Take your time in the beginning, and you'll save yourself lots of energy (and money) in the end.

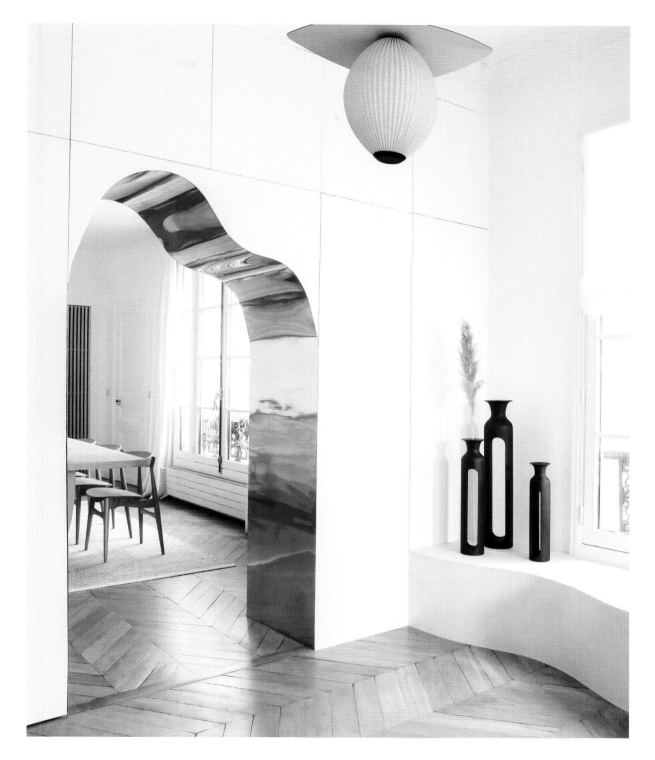

OPPOSITE ABOVE
Texture on texture on more texture (and a rug that follows its own path) add depth – and a little cheekiness – to the all-white mix of this Long Island bedroom I designed for a client.

OPPOSITE BELOW
Keep it neutral. Keep it chic. In any other color, these sculptural walls would look like they belong in a kid's playroom, not a grown-up dining space.

ABOVE
When I say a single wow moment can change your whole perspective, this is what I mean. Without that stunning brass-trimmed doorway this space, designed by Paris-based Heju Studio, would be very beautiful, very traditional, and very mainstream.

OMBRÉ, ALL DAY

That heading could be my mantra because these rooms make me so happy.

Tie-dye. Inkblots. Wild, spiraling colors. These dying techniques take me straight back to the eighties. My sister and I would have weekend tie-dying dates with our mom. Once we figured out the process, there wasn't a white garment in the house safe from our epic rubber-banding skills. I still get that same sense of creative joy when I use a fabric or wallpaper covered in one of these magical prints. Though, these days, my preferred palette is far more *palatable* than my primary rainbow explorations from childhood.

What I love about both of these projects, with the ombré wall and the dip-dyed cabinet curtains, is that they manage to keep the pattern's artful spirit intact. They feel imperfect and handmade — which is especially true of the eating nook. The work of Columbus, Ohio, artist Adam Brouillette, the space was hand-sprayed for actor Debby Ryan and musician Josh Dun's fantastical home.

I talked about the importance of switching up your perspective earlier in this chapter, and this is another example of just how good the results can be when you do. The next time you approach a wall with a can of paint, don't let the goal be to simply coat it evenly. Is this the place for a mural? Could you do an ombré treatment? What if you painted a tiny little scene in a mostly hidden corner that became pure magic for your kids? Tap into your Creative Flow and give it a go.

OPPOSITE
Electric magenta is a bold choice . . . and I love it. This ombré effect would be so great for an entryway or powder room, or even flipped on its head with the gradient dripping down from the ceiling. Painter's choice.

BELOW
I've never held an actual desk job, but the kitchenette in designer Patricia Bustos's Madrid office just might convince me to take one. The latticework bricks from Maora Ceramic are amazing, but it's the ombré cabinet curtains that bring the little gathering space to life.

FOR THE RULE BREAKERS
Who says a doorframe needs molding? Certainly not French interior designer Pierre Yovanovitch, who has made wildly painted ceilings and colorfully splashed doorways a calling card of sorts. Side note: This squiggly pattern works just as well surrounding an unframed piece of art on the wall.

RIGHT
Here's why you should never underestimate the magic that can be created with nothing more than some paint and a roller — and about a thousand yards of painter's tape. Studio Rhonda dreamed up four different geometric "color-scapes" for each of the stairwells in this London Victorian, and they are all super out-of-the-box cool.

FOLLOWING PAGES
The incredible space on the following pages is in Portland, Oregon, and belongs to the endlessly creative muralist and maker Alex Proba, whose no-fear approach to color and pattern always produces the most vividly awesome results (see page 36 for more on her work). She spent four weeks hand-painting this epic design across her main bedroom and bathroom.

ABOVE
Did you know they make wood stains in colors other than neutral tones (like the soft blue-gray you see in this Sydney kitchen by Arent&Pyke)? Stain, unlike paint, pops the veining in wood grain, adding a cool textural effect. This is a smart way to make budget-friendly wood look high-end.

OPPOSITE

EYE CANDY ALERT
I am forever in awe of artist Annie Morris and her "Stack" sculptures. Each colorfully lumpen sphere is hand-molded, cast in bronze, and painted with raw pigment before being assembled into a precarious tower of triumph and joy.

WHAT'S YOUR VIBE?

THE SPACE HEALER

The kids want a wrestling ring. You need a family room.
Is there a middle ground?

When my family and I bought this mid-century ranch back in 2020, the basement had not seen an upgrade since the early sixties. The walls were covered in wood paneling, the floors were parquet, and I kid you not, there was a plastic accordion door stretching from one end of the room to the other. They could have filmed an episode of *Stranger Things* down there.

We immediately knew this space would be the kids' zone, but what that meant looked very different depending on who you asked. Dean and I wanted a spot to lounge for family movie nights. Our sons, Cash and Lennon — who were four and eight years old, respectively, at the time — were more in the market for a wrestling ring. So, my challenge was: How do I marry two creative visions in a way that makes everyone happy, and hopefully minimizes the number of urgent care visits in my life?

As much as I wanted to veto the wrestling ring idea on principle alone, the truth was . . . they were going to wrestle. I could either let them continue to toss each other off their bunk beds and hope for the best, or I could create a room of mostly soft surfaces that would make the impact less terrifying (for me). After a major gut renovation, where I reworked the space's footprint — a laundry room and storage closet were added — and brought the surfaces

into the twenty-first century, I started my design from the ground up.

The custom shearling rug was created with Stark to look like a paint splatter spreading across the floor. I know what you're thinking, "A white rug in a kids' playroom, is she nuts?" Yes, but thankfully natural fibers are surprisingly easy to clean — and our "no shoes inside" policy helps, too. One wall is lined with built-in cabinetry that hides hundreds of games (of the board and video variety), friend sleepover gear, and all our movie-night snacking essentials, including a pullout microwave for popcorn and refrigerator drawers for beverages. Hung across another wall are funny quotes the boys said when they were little, which I had printed on a poster and framed — and will cherish forever.

Then there was the issue of the wrestling ring. Since an actual ring wasn't really conducive to movie watching, I settled on a sofa that doubles as one. This modular configuration is something I designed with Nathan Anthony Furniture, and it is the best investment I've ever made. Covered in a durable velvet, the kids pull it apart to make forts. It has slept half a dozen small humans at one time. And yes, it is frequently used for wrestling . . . usually on top of Dean and I as we attempt to watch a movie.

"I love the sound of smells."

October 1st 201

"We should get a talking cat named Pretzel."

July 5th 2018

"I don't want pizza, I just want Skittles."

January 22th 2021

Want to see the unbelievable before shots? Snap here.

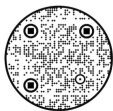

THIS IS YOUR WORLD

THE HAND FEELS . . .

Unexpected textural layers.

Chunky fabrics.

Shearling underfoot.

Velvet-y wallpaper.

THE NOSE SMELLS . . .

Fresh herbs.

Ripe figs.

The salty breeze of the Mediterranean shoreline.

THE EARS HEAR . . .

The first four beats of that song you've been waiting for all night. You know the one.

THE EYES SEE . . .

Architectural moments that sing.

Pigmented wood stains.

Furniture with something to say.

THE SPIRIT CONNECTS . . .

With the trailing stems of a burro's tail succulent.

With citrine for energy and inspiration.

CREATIVE FLOW

ALWAYS
STONED

For all the rock lovers out there. Geologic stripes. Fluid shapes.
Unexpected applications. Let's dig in.

PREVIOUS PAGE
The former Los Angeles bathroom
of Sean Rad and Lizzie Grover Rad,
by interior designer Jane Hallworth,
is the visual definition of luxury.
A calm space wrapped in Breccia
Capraia marble that feels like a
Zen retreat.

ABOVE
A Lina Bo Bardi stool. A custom
vanity by Richard Wakamoto. That
amazing vintage cabinet, found
at Galerie Half. The mid-century
furniture lineup in this bathroom is
as impressive as the stone walls
that contain it. But what's more
important is the contrast it provides.
All that well-worn wood adds
warmth to a space that could come
across as cold.

OPPOSITE
The Rads' steam shower features a
full marble chaise lounge beneath
a vintage brass pendant by Alvar
Aalto. That undulating seat is the
sort of detail that looks so beautiful
and simple but takes a highly skilled
fabricator weeks to get just right.

Look around your house. What's the oldest thing you own? If you have any sort of natural stone surface, there's your answer. It takes thousands of years for these "fancy rocks" to form in the wild. I don't want to spend too much time on the science behind it all, but to grasp how miraculous it is that we even have these materials, you have to understand a little about how they're made.

Marble is essentially the butterfly of the stone world. It's a metamorphic rock that starts out as limestone, and after thousands—sometimes millions—of years of exposure to heat and pressure, becomes marble. All those distinct veins that make this stone so amazing are created when minerals crystalize and recrystallize within the original limestone, like a visual timeline of its formation. Onyx, in contrast, with its wavy bands and translucent nature isn't created by heat, but water. Those undulating lines that make it so unique are actually thousands of years of compounded calcite deposits left behind at the point where groundwater comes to the Earth's surface. The variations between the layers are a centuries-old map of that location's water flow. Seriously, how amazing is our planet?

The rarity of stone—its beauty, its limited quantities—make it the most special thing you can add to a space, whether in little bits or big chunks. The sprawling Los Angeles bathroom you saw on the previous pages happens to be an awesomely over-the-top example of the latter. Interior designer

Jane Hallworth wrapped nearly every square inch of built-in surface in slabs of Breccia Capraia, an Italian marble shot through with deep purple and green veining. Even the cornice above the curtains on page 149 is stone.

I can't underscore enough the amount of work that went into making this space happen. You may think an all-marble bathroom is as easy as finding a stone you love and, essentially, cocooning yourself in it. I'm afraid it's not that simple, though. There are at least a half-dozen people involved before that stone you picked makes it from the slab yard to your home: an interior designer, stone masons, fabricators, installers . . . even specialty movers and equipment are required.

Then there are all the decisions and sourcing that has to happen. To get the sort of continuous pattern you see on these walls, you have to purchase slabs that are book-matched, meaning they were consecutively cut from the same quarry so that when you place them side-by-side the veining aligns. If you want a marble tub, on the other hand, you don't even look at slabs. It must be carved from a single *block* of stone.

I don't say this to deter you. I say it to prepare you—for the cost and the highly involved process. So plan your budget, find your patience, and remember that old song by The Dramatics, "Good Things Don't Come Easy."

DOUBLE DOWN, I DARE YOU

I get this question from people all the time: Can I mix different types of stone in the same space? My answer: Yes, go for it!

This concept always trips people up, but really, it's no different than wearing multiple prints at the same time or mixing fabrics in a room. The key is to make sure everything is speaking the same language, that there's a common thread woven through your choices in order to create a visual connection.

The living room you see here is a great example. Located in Hollywood, it's the work of Lia McNairy and Azar Fattahi of the firm LALA Reimagined. A playful approach to pattern helped them pull off this masterful mix. Here's what I mean: The quartzite fireplace — a stone called Azul Mary from Brazil — is crisscrossed with abstract veining, thick in some spots, thin in others. While the striped coffee table (by one of my design heroes, Patricia Urquiola), with its uniform, linear bands of marble, is screaming, "Check me out!" The patterns couldn't be more opposite, but the repetition of that blue-ish green hue is a subtle acknowledgement from one to the other, like they're saying, "Hey, I see you over there. You do your thing, and I'll do mine."

If you're equally in love with speckles and veining, or you can't decide between a few shades of onyx, here is my final word: The only thing better than one piece of amazing natural stone in a room is two — always!

OPPOSITE

EYE CANDY ALERT
The magic of this Hollywood living room started with Patricia Urquiola's Origami Coffee Table. Every design choice made by the team at LALA Reimagined sprang from the inclusion of this one piece of furniture. The design is a nod to the Japanese art of paper folding done in the sturdiest material imaginable. Cheeky? Yes. Absolutely stunning? Also yes.

HEY, WHY SO SERIOUS?

People think of stone as a very reserved material. It's a weighty investment, for sure. And it should be respected, absolutely. It took the Earth thousands of years to make. But that doesn't mean you can't also have some fun with it. My heart sinks a little when I scroll through Instagram and see one pristine, white marble kitchen after the next. The look is timeless. But I always wonder if the person who chose that design made the decision because they really love white marble or because they think they *should* love white marble. Because at some point, the many varieties of Carrara marble became a status symbol, like the Louis Vuitton logo of the stone world.

Take some time and do your research — please! (This is me begging.) If you do, you'll see that most varieties of stone are *not* white. They are colorful; the patterns are unpredictable and unique. This is what makes this material so special, and, I would add, what makes it such a great choice if you're trying to make a moment sing.

Speaking of singing, the little pink kitchen on the opposite page — the Milan home of Nelcya Chamszadeh and Fabrizio Cantoni of the textile company CC-Tapis — is hitting all the high notes. The milky onyx feels alive, like a waterfall is tumbling down the backsplash. It is a bold choice, certainly. But, I would argue, this kitchen is just as timeless as all those immaculate white ones out there — because great design never dates, and this room is unforgettable.

I can feel your self-doubt bubbling to the surface. *But what if I pick something bold and get tired of it?* Well, let me ask you this: What if you pick something bold and you love it forever? What if you pick something that brings you joy every time you see it?

OPPOSITE
Onyx in a kitchen, like the one seen here in Milan, is the closest you can get to using an actual gemstone in your design, and the price reflects that. But here's a little trick I've learned along the way: Save your dream stone for the backsplash, then pick a budget-friendly material — butcher block, concrete, stainless steel — for the countertops.

ABOVE
If you purchase a slab, do your best to use every square inch. A good fabricator can turn leftovers into cabinet pulls, like the ones you see here, or a small decorative tray, even a trash can to match your bathroom walls.

Korean artist Yongjin Han created these stunning tables. Widely known for his hand-tooled stone carvings and sculptures, Han's body of work is a masterclass in the art of paying tribute to stone in its most natural form.

OPPOSITE
A two-thousand-pound boulder in a kitchen is a first for me. But not for Toronto-based Andrea Kantelberg, whose holistic approach to design has led to some awesomely out-of-the-box material choices meant to positively impact a homeowner's health and wellness.

IT'S TIME TO GET LITERAL

After all the slicing and dicing and polishing and fabricating that goes into preparing a slab of stone for the showroom, it is easy to lose the connection with its monolithic origins, the fact that it once had jagged edges, a chunky shape, and was covered in dirt underground. But that's the truth — and I, for one, don't mind a visual reminder of it. Which is exactly what I love about the rooms you see here.

Both incorporate stone in as close to its natural state as possible, but in wildly unexpected ways (which, by now you've probably realized, is just the way I like it). The Manhattan sitting room on this page belongs to David Mann, of MR Architecture and Decor, and his partner, Fritz Karch, an avid collector, and includes two sculptures by Korean artist Yongjin Han: a set of perfectly sliced stones acting as coffee tables. The huge boulder holding up the kitchen countertop on the opposite page (a design by Andrea Kantelberg) is likely stressing the weight limit of those concrete floors, but, wow, is it glorious. Ultimately, I think it's about flipping the script, bringing something earthy and organic (and usually found outdoors) into a clean-lined space as a way of connecting it to nature.

If the idea of communing in nature speaks to you, then roll over to page 68 and make sure you've checked out Good Vibes Only, my chapter on indoor/outdoor living.

ABOVE

Sabine Marcelis's "Stacked" series pairs amazing specimens of onyx with a block of beautifully sheer, single-cast resin to create wild, off-kilter tables. As usual, the artist's play on materiality is spot-on, pitting the natural against the unnatural in the most stunning ways.

OPPOSITE

Nearing the top of my *can you believe this exists!* list is Alessandro Iliprandi and Francis Cordova's "Marble House" in Tuscany. The entire modernist exterior — not to mention most of the interior — is cut from local Verdi Alpi marble. But it is the built-in sofa, which sits on onyx slabs, not marble, that has me weak in the knees.

ARIELLE ASSOULINE-LICHTEN

To say that Arielle Assouline-Lichten is a girl after my own heart would be a *big* understatement. Her design studio, Slash Objects, established in 2016, takes found and recycled materials and creates high-end products and furniture with a major cool factor. She works with everything from discarded tires to recycled PET (or plastic), but her first love has been and always will be stone.

She rescues cast-offs from the local stone yard — chunks of onyx, blocks of travertine, half-used slabs of marble — and pairs them with other materials, like brass or mohair, to create beautiful, functional compositions. "Caring for the environment," says Assouline-Lichten, "starts by diverting waste from the landfills and using sustainable materials that take our planet's well-being into consideration." Each and every piece she creates for the North American market is handmade in New York City so that she can monitor and guarantee a strict adherence to these standards.

Geometric benches that link cubes of travertine with brass framing and a velvet cushion. Light fixtures suspended in midair by a grounding hunk of alabaster. And my favorite, a swinging swath of mohair balanced between two blocks of marble that passes as a chair (see page 196). Her collections poke fun at the concept of gravity and our perception of the tactile experience in general. Soft and hard. Heavy and light. It's all up for interpretation. And from one Always Stoned girl to another, I'm in awe of her boldness.

OPPOSITE
Marble lasts a lifetime, something I always remind my clients. Don't just consider how you'll use it in your initial design, but also how you'll grow with it. I chose Grand Antique marble for this family's powder room, a project in San Diego, because they can change up the tile down the road, even switch out the fixtures if they want, but the stone is never going to date.

ABOVE
This incredible bathtub is part of my collaboration with ABC Stone. You won't find a single sharp edge or corner because I wanted the shape to feel fluid and soft, a contradiction to the hard block of stone it was cut from.

FOLLOWING PAGES
French architect and designer Michel Amar is so skilled at highlighting the natural beauty of whatever stone he happens to be working with. For a client's apartment in Paris, he's taken the rough, often craggy surface of travertine and amplified it, using an exaggerated, puzzle-pieced-together configuration to make a gorgeous – and slightly rugged – dining table.

BLACK + WHITE + RAD ALL OVER

I talked earlier in this chapter about stone that sings, and, well, here's one of my favorites: Grand Antique marble. True to its name, it has a *grand* history. Originating in a river valley in France's Pyrenees mountains, this stone was once favored by the ancient Romans and is seen in architecture throughout Europe. Because it is only found in that particular valley, and only extracted in limited quantities each year, this stone is extremely rare, which – of course – only heightens its cachet.

The unique pattern structure is what makes this stone so special. Instead of wisps of veining, it looks more like it's been embedded with shards of glass. I just have to wonder what sort of natural phenomenon occurred to create those dramatic black and white patches. It reminds me that in design, bold doesn't have to mean bright and colorful and over-the-top. This stone is graphic, mono-chromatic, and, even in small doses – say, as a sink or a bathtub, as shown here – can make a big impact.

ABOVE

FOR THE RULE BREAKERS
This is the Soft Rock Chair, another piece from
my collaboration with ABC Stone. I wanted
to mess around with the characteristics of
marble, try to soften it a bit by pairing it with an
incredibly nubby bouclé fabric. Sit back. Relax.
Turn up the Fleetwood Mac. That's the vibe.

OPPOSITE

I am convinced that French furniture makers
Marbera are having the most fun with this
material, churning out so many gorgeous,
modern pieces, including this space-age
coffee table, which mixes sixties onyx, aged
mirror, and travertine.

THE SPACE HEALER

Marble floors just aren't in the budget. Is there a work-around?

My clients purchased a hundred-year-old home on the beach in New Jersey for every reason you'd expect a person to buy an older home. It had intricate, original moldings. There was a grand entrance. They fell in love with the little nooks and quirky features. All the hallmarks of a traditional Victorian home were in place, except one – the floors.

In keeping with the aesthetics of the era in which this house was built, you would have expected some sort of stately stone floor, especially in the entryway. But instead, we found the tiniest, one-inch-wide floorboards running through most of its rooms. They were so thin and scuffed up, I mistook them for the subflooring, the structural material that goes under your actual floor. It was a pretty big blow to the overall excitement bubble surrounding this place.

In a magical world where I could give my clients whatever they wanted, an entryway with classic, checkered marble floors would have been the request, a period-appropriate choice to match the home's original character. But marble tiles were an out-of-reach investment for them. Telling someone they can't have something they really want is the worst part of my job, a moment I go to great lengths to avoid. So when the inevitable ask came down – could I find a creative way to make a marble-floored entryway happen? – my answer was, "No, but . . . how do you feel about painting one instead?"

My usually up-for-anything clients looked at me as if I'd lost my mind. How could painted floors look elevated? But then I showed them photos of my former flat in London, where the old pine planks had been painted white and looked amazing. They were skeptical but agreed to give it a shot. After all, if they liked it, it would save them thousands of dollars in flooring. If they didn't, they'd be out the cost of a few gallons of paint and minimal labor.

To start, we sanded and prepped the entryway. Then we covered the whole thing in a heavy-duty, high-gloss, white exterior paint. After it dried, we went back and taped off the checkerboard pattern, and painted all those details in high-gloss black. The benefit of using exterior paint is twofold: the durability, of course, but it also goes on extra-thick, which helped mask the lines between floorboards.

It turned out to be a pretty spot-on replication, especially when photographed. But I say that with a bold-faced asterisk attached: In real life, you can absolutely tell these floors are painted, not stone. But fooling people into thinking they were marble was never the point. Finding a way to give my clients a luxury look for less was the goal – and on that front, I would call this a success.

Want to see those
one-inch floorboards
before they were
painted? Snap here.

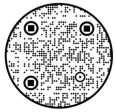

THIS IS YOUR WORLD

THE HAND FEELS . . .

A tactile study of stone finishes, from tumbled to carved to leathered.

THE NOSE SMELLS . . .

Warm, earthy amber chased by a little bit of *you-know-what*.

THE EARS HEAR . . .

Soft echoes.

THE EYES SEE . . .

What they want! Forms taking shape in the abstract lines of a stone's pattern.

Streamlined silhouettes.

Vintage wood and texture-rich fabrics.

THE SPIRIT CONNECTS . . .

With the twisting trunk of a fan aloe tree.

With petrified wood to encourage personal transformation.

ALWAYS STONED

CLEAN
SLATE

Minimalism—with toppings. Function first. Calming colors.
Clean sight lines. A lighter mental load.

PREVIOUS PAGE
Welcome to the kids' pantry in my kitchen. I get a contact high from its level of organization. Everything from the breakfast cereal to the snacks have clear, individual containers, so I know when it's time to order more. Plus, those deep, back-of-the-cabinet-door shelves hold water bottles and overflow groceries.

ABOVE
Refrigerated drawers hidden behind cabinet fronts house drinks, fruit, yogurt, you name it. It is all about ease and function. But, as an added bonus, my kids no longer stand at the main fridge, doors flung open for ten minutes, waiting for food that isn't there to appear.

BELOW
A drawer within a drawer is such a brilliant invention. I was able to squeeze in double the snacks — and keep everything super-organized — by adding a sliding tier to this extra-deep drawer. This config-uration actually costs slightly less than building two shallower individual ones.

OPPOSITE
I carried over the hardware and cabinet style from the rest of my kitchen to visually connect this little nook — which sits off to the side in a small hallway — with the rest of the room.

Function first is a design principle I live by. No matter the project. No matter the mood. No matter the potential scope. Who you are. What's important to you. How you want to live in your home. These *have* to be your primary considerations. Before color palettes, before style, before furniture, and, I would even argue, before you buy or rent a home. Skip this pivotal self-knowledge stage, and you could create the most beautiful living room in the world *that no one in your family wants to sit in*, or the kitchen of your dreams *with no spot to store your favorite mug.*

If you are a Clean Slate devotee, however, you take this idea of organization even more seriously. Function is not only number one on your list; it is also numbers two, three, four, and five. That's because you find what's going on behind the scenes—inside cabinets, drawers, closets—just as exciting as all the design elements that are front and center. (A place for everything and everything in its place. Am I right?) Outsiders may conflate this infatuation with neatness as a need for control, but, in actuality, it is a need for sanity—and keeping yours intact.

In my experience, the type of person who wants a Clean Slate space is managing a weighty mental load, to borrow a term from author Eve Rodsky. (And, for the sake of calling a spade a spade— it's likely an overcommitted mom like me.) They are attempting the unenviable act of having to juggle work *and* kids *and* running a household *and* life, and this hyper-organization is what keeps everything flowing. Not having to spend five minutes searching for a pen with ink. Not wrestling with piles of clothes on the floor because the drawers are full. Not having a million little things on display that need to be dusted and styled and fiddled with. By taking these potential time-sucks out of the equation, indispensable minutes of the day are being reclaimed.

"What will make my life easier?" was the question I was asking myself when—poof!—I came up with the idea of creating a completely separate kid's pantry in my kitchen. *Mom, can I have something to eat? Mom, I need something to drink! Mom, feed me!* I don't want to attempt to add up the amount of time I have spent answering the whims of my sons' stomachs. This entire pantry was designed to help them help themselves. It is situated across from a highly trafficked side entrance to our house. All their food and drinks are organized and accessible so they can grab what they need whether they're coming or going.

I know I talked about sanity before, but when I tell you this pantry is a big reason why I'm still holding on to mine—at least most of it—it is not an exaggeration.

…BUT NEVER A BORE

Just because you're letting function lead doesn't mean you have to leave creativity behind. Both can (and should) exist in your spaces. Sure, you've considered and planned every square inch of viable storage in the places you can't see — and, exhale, that feels awesome. But what's your plan for the places you *can* see?

It's okay to keep it simple. In my kitchen, the rule is: Nothing stays on the counter that isn't serving a daily purpose. But you still need those design moments that pop. If you're looking for a minimal effort, maximum impact solution, then color and texture are where you want to spend your time and money.

Take the kitchen on the facing page, located in LA's Silver Lake neighborhood, a design by And And And Studio, where the combination of fern green cabinets and a fluted wood island surround is enough to make this space pop. There's also an awesomely unexpected play on scale happening. The marble backsplash only travels halfway up the wall, while the exaggerated pendant light is hung extra low. Together, they drop the sightlines, making the room feel cozy and intimate, despite its soaring ceilings.

OPPOSITE
How good is this circular island? It was designed by (and belongs to) Annie Ritz and Daniel Rabin. A kid-friendly lack of sharp corners and all that hidden, under-the-counter storage make it practical. But, like a round dining table, it has a come-hang-out-around-me magnetic pull when people are over.

THAT'S A NO FOR ME

People often think adding personality to a room means filling it with accessories: art, family photos, ceramics, books, throw pillows, and on it goes. The tale of you in 102 items. But that's not so. If you're a true minimalist, even the idea of all that stuff is a big n-o for you. Personal touches can be just that . . . touches. Small, unexpected details that make a functional item — a sofa, a coffee table, a light fixture — interesting.

In the living room shown here, you can count the number of pieces it holds on two hands. But it *feels* totally lived in. It has a vibe and a point of view. And that's because there is nothing basic about those handfuls of items. The ottoman with its wavy edges, the mirror with its organic border, those extra-thick throw pillows, even the wispy, barely-there olive tree — each and every item has a story to tell.

Now, full disclosure, this is a campaign shot from Lulu and Georgia's collaboration with spatial designer Eny Lee Parker, who created the amazing ottoman you see. That doesn't make it less of an inspirational moment for your home, though — and it certainly hasn't stopped half a dozen clients from sending me this photo as part of their mood board.

OPPOSITE
Talk about low maintenance. This Lulu and Georgia sofa, with its tight, clean lines, is a zero-fluffing-required investment. I can imagine kids and pets jumping on it one minute, guests sipping martinis the next.

The bar in my home is a nook inside a larger lounge area. When I have people over, they ask about the stools (they're by Interlude Home), the wallpaper (Abstraction 504 by Fabricut), the sconce on the wall (SkLO). But my favorite detail is also the smallest. The thin brass strip running through the side of the marble countertop is, for me, the moment that ties this whole space together.

FOR THE RULE BREAKERS

I'm all for a mismatched seating scenario. But when you add a sofa to the mix, you're leveling up on that idea. You can find a clean-lined, modern one like this for less than the cost of four more of those ladderback chairs. The vibe is inviting and so cozy—which might be why designers Homan Rajai and Elena Dendiberia, of Studio Ahead in San Francisco, hung an upholstered headboard on the wall as art.

OH, HELLO THERE

Let's talk about entryways. When it comes to creating mood, this space often gets a bum deal. Blame budget. Blame square footage. Blame a lack of energy and time. I get it. You can only do so much. But hear me out because . . . entryways are so important!

Studies have shown it takes between seven seconds and two minutes for a person to form a first impression. This means that unless your guests are sprinting from the front door to whatever room you are entertaining in, that first impression is happening in your entryway. It doesn't matter that you have a newly renovated kitchen. It doesn't matter that you just reupholstered your custom 18-foot sofa in the most amazing fabric ever. If I walk in and see a pile of dirty sneakers and an overflowing coat rack, *that* is the vibe imprinting on my brain.

Technically, the vignette you see here is not an entryway. It's the gorgeous side table of interior designer Kelly Behun's Southampton bedroom. But it has all the makings of a perfect entryway moment. A little something happening on the wall. A console with a drawer for stashing things—mail, keys, sunglasses, etc. Fresh flowers and a stunning light. Think about how amazing it would feel to come home to this view. No tower of shoes. No mountain of coats. Just a moment of beauty to set the right tone.

Great idea, but what am I supposed to do with all the coats and shoes? I can feel your ire. Stop stressing and flip the page for some thoughts on stylish storage solutions.

OPPOSITE
The fluted wood backdrop in Kelly Behun's home is such a brilliant idea. You could buy individual rods or paneled moldings to design your own geometric masterpiece. Though, if that sounds too challenging, companies like Urban Wallcovering make peel-and-stick slats out of real wood that require less DIY skills.

WHAT'S YOUR VIBE?

Entryways lined in cabinets are not my favorite. But I get why people do it – all that glorious storage. Here's the thing, though: You can do a bank of cupboards while still adding personality. Instead of a wall of boring cabinet doors, think about ways to make those doors pop. Could you add an unexpected diagonal slash and a porthole, like you see here (brilliant additions by Gundry + Ducker for a project in London)? Or get creative with paint?

Now, about those shoes that need a home by the front door. Interior designer Rafael de Cárdenas created this channeled banquette and tiered marble built-in for clients in Paris. What makes it perfect entryway inspo, though, are the extra-deep bottom drawers. You could create something similar out of a less pricey material. Picture it: Click-and-close drawers you tap with your toe, a shoe filing system inside – it's pure organizational bliss.

JEPPE CHRISTENSEN

Challenge: Design a warm and inviting kitchen that is streamlined yet high-functioning — and, of course, beautiful and budget-friendly and as sustainable as possible.

Just your standard request from every client on every kitchen project I've ever worked on. I've always had to approach this ask with a weighing of wishes and an eventual compromise. But that's not the case for Copenhagen-based cabinetry company Reform, whose answer, since its founding in 2014, has always been: *Sure, we can do that.*

"Great kitchen design had always been exclusionary, expensive, and out of reach for regular people," explains Jeppe Christensen, Reform's founder and current creative director. So Christensen, along with his partner Michael Andersen, set out to make a company that did things differently, channeling a less-is-more approach and creating a system that is modular, responsibly made, and ticks off an incredibly versatile checklist of needs. (Want a place to store your cheese knives? There's a drawer for that.) All of this while maintaining a reasonable price range.

But can Scandinavian minimalism still be, well, interesting? I talked to Christensen about this, and he said it's a matter of personal taste, and the key is "finding the right balance between contrasting elements." Meaning, if you have a clean, simple layout, choose vibrant colors or unexpected materials, and vice-versa. A bolder floor plan should be met with soothing tones and natural materials. Whatever the combination, the good news is there are more options than ever before at Reform, from mirrored fronts to rainbow hues — and they now have seven showrooms open Stateside where you can see them all. My advice: Figure out function first, then have some fun.

WHAT'S YOUR VIBE?

Part of a loft in Rotterdam inhabited by Dutch artist Sabine Marcelis, her partner, architect Paul Cournet, and their son, Koa, this minimalist bedroom exudes calmness. The design choices don't simply feel like an accumulation of cool objects. They seem to exist as a physical answer to how they, as a family, want to live and move through this space.

EYE CANDY ALERT
In terms of form, this industrial sink is all function. But when the design team at Balbek Bureau decided to take it and dip it in matte brass for a nail salon in Kyiv, they really created a piece that sings. You could re-create this look by taking an old metal tub to your local finishing shop.

WELCOME TO YOUR HAPPY PLACE

If Clean Slate is your world, then the closet is where you head to unwind, your favorite spot to flex some organizational muscle.

Now, as convenient as it is to pop into a one-stop closet shop or pick up a system from IKEA and call it a day, the real magic happens when you level-up an off-the-shelf offering and really make it work for you. The first step to doing that is taking stock of what you need. You have a thing for jewelry. *Great.* At last count, you owned 106 belts. *No judgment here.* Your scarf collection could fill its own closet. *I'm impressed.*

But if you're going to own a lot of little things, you need a plan and a place to store them. Otherwise, they end up in an unnavigable pile. (I speak from experience.) Don't worry, the solution is not running out and spending tens of thousands of dollars on a fully custom closet. That, thankfully, is unnecessary. But my advice *is* to go custom, at least when it comes to organizational add-ons: drawer dividers, shelf separators, bins, and shoe risers.

All of these made-to-order pieces are now available on Etsy. There are so many highly skilled woodworkers on that platform, even local talent, who will build to the exact specifications of your closet. So just like the fully custom versions, every square inch of space is accounted for, and every bow tie, shoe clip, and sun hat has a home.

OPPOSITE
In their London Victorian, Jordan Cluroe and Russell Whitehead, the team behind 2LG Studio, upgraded a bank of shelving with a wavy frame and an electric-yellow curtain instead of doors, both of which are easy lifts that make such an impact.

DO THE TWIST

When you're so focused on the what-goes-where of it all, it's easy to overlook an opportunity for a great design moment—but don't! Yes, the goal is minimal and orderly, but it is not copy-and-paste. That means not rushing through the creative process for the sake of having a finished room. It means slowing down long enough to find pieces that you connect with, investment pieces that have a little something extra going on, whether that's a material used in an unexpected way, like the travertine furniture you see on this page, or a finishing touch that kicks things up a notch (a brass button, a saturated color). Give yourself the time you need, and enjoy the thrill of the hunt.

OPPOSITE LEFT
New York-based designer/architect Arielle Assouline-Lichten uses recycled materials and stone remnants to create her Adri Chair. A nod to the iconic sling chairs of the mid-1900s, this seat takes that concept and ups the fun by a hundred. To learn more about her work, flip to page 162.

OPPOSITE RIGHT
I love the almost trompe-l'œil effect of this coffee table, another design by French furniture maker Arthur Vallin. It looks as if the stone were heated up — like marshmallow — stretched long, and folded in half. In actuality, it was hand-carved from a single piece of Travertine Navona.

ABOVE
This console's brilliance hinges on the addition of the brass pin. Another cheeky design by Arthur Vallin, it feels like that single bauble is the only thing holding this table together. Remove it, and gravity would quickly do its thing.

THE SPACE HEALER

Does Asian bath culture exist in Long Island? It does at this house.

A few years ago, a neighbor came to me with a question I'd never been asked before — a rare occurrence after two decades of doing what I do. She wanted to know if I could transform their very traditional main bathroom into an Asian-inspired, spa-like retreat. She explained that her husband, a fashion executive, was spending a lot of time in that part of the world for work and was taken with the bathing culture in Japan. My answer was, "Yes, of course, let's do it." Then I had to figure out what I'd just agreed to.

What I didn't know at the time was that in Japan, taking a bath is not simply what you do at the end of the day to get the grime off. (I admit, I had a lot to learn.) It's a leisurely, meditative, daily routine . . . with steps. Homes have bathing rooms dedicated to this ritual. These spaces typically have big, deep tubs, a window, a wall-mounted shower, and a place to sit down. You enter, soap up, relax, shower off, relax, take a soak, relax — you get the picture. My muscles start untangling just thinking about it.

These bathing rooms are very minimal and very Zen, and as much as this couple wanted their en suite to function like the traditional Japanese versions that inspired them, they also wanted very modern, very luxurious materials and finishes (marble, walnut,

Apparatus light fixtures). So, my challenge became: how to bring a little East-meets-West magic to Long Island.

I reconfigured the space to give them a generous water room, which was outfitted with a freestanding tub, two showerheads, a hand shower, and a wall of jets that were custom-placed to the specifications of my client's pressure points. There are paneled mirrors above the vanity that amplify the natural light coming from a window on the wall opposite the shower. And I had the faucet and lighting mounted directly onto the mirror to keep everything streamlined. There's even open shelving for rolled towels, like you would find in a spa.

Nothing beats experiencing the real thing, of course. But I did pull off something pretty close, bringing the spirit of Japanese bathing culture halfway around the world while giving a busy exec a much-needed place to unwind.

Curious about
the un-Zen-like
atmosphere that
preceded this
update? Snap here to
see the before shot.

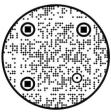

THIS IS YOUR WORLD

THE HAND FEELS . . .

Over-stuffed upholstery.

Fluted wood.

Brass, leather, and travertine.

THE NOSE SMELLS . . .

Fresh laundry.

Linen.

A hint of citrus.

THE EARS HEAR . . .

Silence — what bliss.

THE EYES SEE . . .

Order everywhere.

Neutral palettes shot through
with pale hues.

Clean lines broken up by
exaggerated forms.

THE SPIRIT CONNECTS . . .

With the feathery branches
of an olive tree.

With clear quartz for clarity and
concentration.

CLEAN SLATE

PINK

Dynamic lessons in layering. Shaded undertakings.
Rapid mood swings. Try to keep up.

PREVIOUS PAGE
Consider your sightlines. Notice how the fluting on the wall in this Madrid apartment designed by Patricia Bustos jumps from floor-to-ceiling in the kitchen to only covering half the wall in the dining room. The sharp vertical lines act like a frame for all those beautiful, curvy design details on the banquette.

ABOVE
Countertops with shock value are among my greatest design loves. Pink terrazzo shot through with emerald green shards is the last thing I would expect to find in this kitchen, which makes it such a brilliant choice.

BELOW
Pick your moments. Everything in a room should not be wildly expensive. Sure, this eat-in kitchen is flanked by custom furniture, but the floors are cement, the banquet lighting is a series of exposed bulbs in simple fixtures, and that rattan pendant (from Home by Auk) couldn't be more wallet-friendly.

OPPOSITE
Nicknamed Casa Olá or "house of waves," this pint-size apartment had an unexciting blocky layout before Bustos reimagined the whole space, creating soft breaks and curving silhouettes around its borders to redirect flow with a thoughtful, energetic pace between rooms.

You: Can a single color *really* encapsulate an entire mood? Me: Absolutely. For sure. One hundred percent yes!

Because here's the interesting thing about pink: It's a chameleon. As much as people like to assign it a gender, I think it's completely fluid. It can be feminine. It can be masculine. It's just very cool—always.

Now, for those of you still grumbling about pink being a color for young girls or Barbie, here's a quick history lesson: If the year were 1918, and you had a son, he would be wearing pink. It was considered a "stronger color" than blue, according to an article printed that year in a popular trade publication called *The Infants' Department*. You would also be wearing pink if you were a well-off European man in the 1700s, to symbolize your social status and wealth (insert massive eye roll here).

Obviously, all that color versus gender versus social hierarchy symbolism is a bunch of B.S. But what I think is and always has been true of the color pink is that it is powerful. It vibrates with confidence, steals all the attention, leaves an impression. I am instinctively drawn to this shade. It soothes me. You'll see it over and over again in the spaces I create—an impulse I share with Patricia Bustos, an interior designer out of Spain, and the woman who created the pink utopia seen on the previous pages.

The eat-in kitchen ticks all my boxes for this mood: It's powerfully pink, exudes total confidence, and when it comes to impressions, it certainly leaves a lasting one. The homeowners' brief for Bustos included a request that the entire apartment, which is located in Madrid, be inspired by the sea. In the wrong hands, a demand like that could go very, very wrong. But instead, Bustos steered their vision in a beautifully elevated direction, layering curving organic shapes with imperfect finishes; playing natural elements, like bamboo and rattan, against luxe velvet and nubby bouclé; and wrapping the whole space in shades of pale pink.

This color can be a lot of things, including, apparently, a magical apartment that feels as if it belongs under the sea. Still, it isn't a mood for everyone. Tip too far in any direction—everything light pink or hyper-hot pink or not enough design diversity, for instance—and there is serious danger of falling into the stereotypical tropes associated with this shade. Millennial pink café or Barbie's Dreamhouse are not the goals here.

But for those of us who do feel its cosmic pull, pink is a happy place to orbit, one filled with unique mashups, masterful layering, and plenty of space for personal interpretation.

THE WEIGHT
OF PINK

Here's the thing about pink: A little can feel like a lot — and that's not necessarily a bad thing. Take this bedroom, for instance. I designed it for The Holiday House Hamptons showhouse in 2019. It got a ton of press, was all over Instagram, and every single person who wrote about it referred to it as "the pink bedroom." If you zoomed out, though, you'd see there is exactly one design element in this entire space that's pink . . . the walls. Everything else — the bed, the bedding, the rug, the nightstands, the dresser, all of it — is white.

To be fair, I get that blush-toned inkblot wallpaper isn't exactly subtle. But the unconscious magnification of its color speaks to my point. It's this illusory quality, the ability to fool the eye and feel bigger than it is, that makes this shade so much fun to play with — especially if you're unsure how far you want to take it. You don't have to go all out to *go all out*. A stair runner or even a single, stunning lamp or ceramic sculpture might be enough for you. Though, if that little voice in your head is telling you to cover every available surface in pink, please know I fully support that, too.

OPPOSITE
Forget the lipstick; I like a message etched directly into the mirror. I design these personalized glass surfaces for clients sometimes, and they include everything from a positive mantra to a sweet line of poetry — a thoughtful touch and a bit of whimsy that go a long way.

ABOVE
As part of my creative process, I always ask myself: How can I break open an everyday object, put it back together, and come up with something new? That is exactly what the team at AKZ Architectura accomplished with this staircase. Lining its pink runner with a mirrored border made the whole structure look as if it was floating in mid-air.

FOLLOWING PAGES
The curves. The perfect shade of pink. The cozy mohair velvet fabric. Everything about the sophisticated sitting room in Ulla Johnson's Manhattan showroom, a design by Rafael de Cárdenas, says come in and make yourself comfortable.

IT'S OK TO BE SHADY SOMETIMES

I love millennial pink, don't get me wrong. It's light. It's happy. It's versatile. But it's also been done to near death. (The last time I googled "millennial pink," I got over 104 million results.) I'm not saying don't use it. I still do — all the time. What I am saying is . . . don't let it be the *only* pink you use in a space. There's a whole spectrum of spectacular pinks, from blush to burgundy, and each one brings its own unique energy to a design.

Warmer than white and gray, more crisp than taupe, lighter shades of pink can be incredibly soothing and work so well as an alternative to your standard neutrals. Deeper tones — think amaranth and rose — feel bolder and more mature.

The real design magic happens when you layer them all together, though. You get depth, dimension, and texture — you get a room that sings. Here's a good rule of thumb: The more diverse your spectrum, the more funk you bring. Meaning, pairing the very light with the very bright, for instance, is going to be more dramatic than playing around with a bunch of shades that are a similar tone.

The rooms you see on this page are great examples. The coffee table on this page has a dozen shades of pink, from salmon to fuchsia — a mix that keeps your eye moving from object to object, and around again. In contrast, the bedroom's approach feels more purposeful — a few well-chosen pops of rose that jump out against its pretty, muted walls.

ABOVE
EYE CANDY ALERT
Each time I see these jewel-toned Lucite orbs by Fenton & Fenton, they pull me in. Tonally, they were made to be pink's punchier sidekick, and when the sun hits the center, it's as if they glow.

OPPOSITE
If the thought of picking the perfect palette is causing an anxiety spike, follow the lead of designer Andrés Gutiérrez, who created all the color-coded rooms at Mexico City's Ignacia Guest House. Give yourself a pale shell to start, then add one additional shade at a time, until the mix feels right to you.

WHAT'S YOUR VIBE?

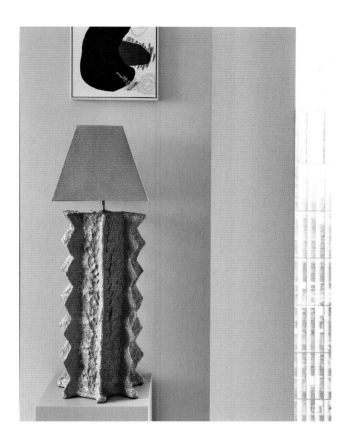

IN THE PRESENCE OF GREATNESS

The next time you add a new piece of furniture or an object to a room, I want you to stop and remember this: Nothing is simply what it appears to be. A lamp should never just be a lamp, a chair never just a chair. Each should serve its primary function, of course, providing light or a place to sit. But when you open your mind to seeing the deeper – often awesomely weird – potential in these everyday objects, what you're *actually* doing is making space for inspiration.

The lampshade that feels too small but is also somehow exactly right. The armchair that resembles a Muppet but makes your heart sing. Out-of-the-box design decisions like these create the ultimate conversation pieces – and I don't mean between you and your dinner guest who wants a house tour. I mean a conversation between you and the object itself. Our best design choices, whether pink or any other shade, talk back, inviting us to pause and contemplate their many eccentric details. I always say, the more an object stops you in your tracks, the more your connection with that object will deepen. Along the way, your home becomes much more personal, too.

So the next time you see something unusual – an asymmetrical silhouette or an off-kilter pattern – I give you permission to run towards it with open arms.

RIGHT

FOR THE RULE BREAKERS
Tile countertops, love them or (seriously) hate them, there is a lesson to be learned here, and it's this: Magenta in a kitchen is a great idea. Also, tiling an island, like this one designed by Antwerp-based Jill Rooijakkers — even if you swapped out the top for solid stone or butcher block — is such a great way to get a lot of visual bang for your buck.

ABOVE

EYE CANDY ALERT

Davide Medri's "Freedom Light" is a chain link/
disco ball hybrid — and now my life is complete.
Each link is lined with its own strip of lighting,
so in this powder room I designed for a
client in Miami, it works in lieu of traditional
vanity fixtures.

OPPOSITE

A pink surprise tucked behind a wall of
cabinetry, this hidden vanity in Melbourne,
designed by Thomas Mckenzie, was a request
by the homeowner so multiple people could
get ready in the bathroom at the same time.
Whatever the reason, I love sneaky pops of
color that jump out of unexpected places —
drawers, closets, cabinets . . . get creative.

PINK POWER MOVES, WATCH OUT

Could there be a more boss color for a home office? Sure, once-upon-a-1980s film, pink was associated exclusively with girly-girl energy and therefore relegated to closets, powder rooms, and nurseries. But here's the thing: That particular bubble popped, and the 2010s were holding the needle responsible.

Pink is not just for pretty spaces that should be seen but not lived in. At the height of her reign at J.Crew, Jenna Lyons sat at a watermelon pink desk. Kelly Wearstler designed an office featuring peach-hued walls and raspberry chairs nearly a decade ago. And everyone from writer/editor Tavi Gevinson to actor/comedian Jessica Williams frequented the once-pink halls of The Wing's co-working spaces in New York City and Los Angeles.

I say all that to make this very important point: Pink is a power player. It's a motivator, a source of inspiration, a sign that you're not afraid to make bold choices — in design and in life. I need that sort of energy from the place I go each day to get things done. I have to *want* to be there. Otherwise, procrastination sets in and you'll find me cleaning bathroom tile with a toothbrush rather than answering client emails.

Don't get me wrong, I'm not saying painting your office pink will automatically make you hyper-efficient. I wish it were that easy. What I am saying is that setting up an inspiring place to work, pink or otherwise, is setting yourself up for success. It could be as simple as lighting a candle (in which case, may I recommend something with cedarwood, which helps with mental clarity) or surrounding yourself with white (or pink!) noise. No matter the catalyst — paint color, scent, sound — carve out a space for it and make a ritual around it, wherever you happen to go to tick off those to-dos.

OPPOSITE
Speaking of inspiring places to work . . . this pink marble desk is a dream. The London-based team at Bohinc Studio designed their Kipferl desk during the pandemic with a curving shape that mimics the Austrian pastry it is named for. (I mean, who wasn't carb-loading from their computer at that time?)

BELOW
Nothing ruins my creative flow faster than piles of loose paper or a stapler without a home, which is why closed storage in an office is a must. The varying shapes, shades, and sizes of these stackable cabinets, a design by Norwegian architect Andreas Nygaard, are an incredibly sophisticated play on color and millwork.

STUDIO VISIT
HELLE MARDAHL STUDIO

HELLE MARDAHL

Helle Mardahl creates eye candy inspired by actual candy in a studio she calls her "candy universe." In case you were wondering why I love her, that sentence explains it all. Her colorful, mouth-blown glass creations, each with its own perfectly imperfect shape, are both temptingly playful and wildly fragile. Having grown up in a home dominated by architectural minimalism, the multi-faceted Danish designer developed her colorful lexicon early on. It was her own personal technicolor revolt.

What started with a lineup of tonally exciting glass dishes, cups, and vases back in 2017 — a series she now calls her Bon Bon Signatures — has expanded into lighting, hardware, and a full collection of tableware, which, for obvious reasons, includes some very cool candy dishes. She also happens to speak fluent "pink." You'll find dozens of shades, from milky rose to fruit punch. "I aim to find the hues of pink that remind me of a flavor," she says. "Strawberry bubblegum, rhubarb from the garden, a spicy red chile, or a perfect sweet-and-sour grapefruit; connecting a hue with a taste makes everything more sensuous and delicious." In other words, her designs are good enough to eat. But you shouldn't . . . because they're glass, obviously.

THE SPACE HEALER

Four white walls of boringness in a can't-touch-them rental.
Where can you have a little fun?

My client Robyn Blair Lazer, the fiery woman behind fine art brand by robynblair, creates candy-themed pop art for a living. Her signature large-scale Lucite boxes are stuffed with sugary childhood treats – Dubble Bubble, pink Starburst, Blow Pops, you name it – each with its own hilarious statement printed across the front: "Warning Sugar High," for instance, or my all-time favorite, "Break in Case of Emergency." That's to say, aesthetically, she isn't afraid of color, and she has a pretty healthy sense of humor.

When I met her back in 2019, she was in the middle of turning a very small bedroom in her (now former) Tribeca apartment into a home office. But she'd hit a roadblock – a common one in NYC: She wasn't allowed to make any major changes to the space. It was a rental, and it was temporary. So, painting walls only to repaint them white was not an investment she wanted to make. Nor was removable wallpaper, which we all know runs a serious risk of ripping off the top layer of your wall. Her plea to me was this: Help me make this room feel like me without breaking the rules of my lease.

Functionally, she needed a lot of storage. She also asked for a desk big enough to fit, on occasion, more than one person. Two large requests considering the small footprint. I started by lining an entire wall with a storage system from IKEA, so she would have plenty of drawers to hide awkward-to-organize material samples and cherished candy wrapper ephemera. Because they were white, they blended in with the walls and felt less bulky. For a desk, we ended up bringing in one of her own custom creations, a Lucite table with a Candy Dot pattern printed across the top. It was just the pop of color the space needed, and since the legs were clear, visually, it left a lot of breathing room.

To play up the candy theme, I added a set of bubblegum pink velvet chairs and lined the storage shelves with stacks of Robyn's electric-bright candy dishes alongside beautiful glass apothecary jars filled with actual candy. (Because your strawberry Airheads should always be within arm's reach, right?) Layer on an oversized inkblot rug from Wayfair and entering this room was enough to give you a sugar high.

THIS IS YOUR WORLD

THE HAND FEELS . . .

A tactile playground.

Subtle fluting.

Textured cement.

Super-soft velvet.

Untamable faux fur.

THE NOSE SMELLS . . .

Fresh magnolia and jasmine.

Peppery notes of cardamom.

THE EARS HEAR . . .

The hypnotic thump of your own heartbeat.

THE EYES SEE . . .

A pink party!

Reflective surfaces.

Terrazzo that pops.

Natural materials in contrast.

THE SPIRIT CONNECTS . . .

With the swaying leaves of a bird-of-paradise.

With rose quartz for unconditional love.

PINK

PINK

LET'S GET TO IT

You've connected with your design spirit. You have a better understanding of how your spaces, and the way you live in them, affect your mood. Now what? The chapters that follow are a resource guide like none you've read before. It deals not just in the *basic* elements of interior design — though you'll find an extensive list of my most-trusted vendors on that front. We go deeper than that, cataloging sensory tools, like plants, crystals, colors, and scents, and the nuanced vibes each creates. We look at inspiration: Where to find it. How to save it. These chapters hold everything you need to be confident enough to dust off your overlooked design projects and get started, which, as we all know, is the hardest part.

The diaphanous cloud room in designer Kelly Behune's incredible Manhattan apartment.

THE INSPIRATION GATHERER

. . . because the hunt is a big part of the fun.

———

One of the questions I get asked most is, "How do you find inspiration?" In the moment, I might say something like Pinterest or Instagram or just everyday life. But the simple truth is . . . inspiration can't be distilled down to just one thing. It's a happy (sometimes messy, sometimes extremely organized) amalgamation of all the things. I know, "all the things" feels a bit daunting, but the good news is, there are many ways to inspiration-gather, from the digital to the tangible — and you should try them all.

Magazines, movies, museums, trade shows, travel, shopping trips, catalogs, people you admire, Etsy, Instagram, Pinterest, online rabbit holes, walking through the grocery store — there is inspiration to be found in all of these places, as long as you're looking for it. I grew my social following organically over the last eight years by staying true to my aesthetic and connected to the content I share. And, along the way, I've learned a few tricks to efficiently use the digital world as a tool for finding inspiration — and storing it. Here's what I know . . .

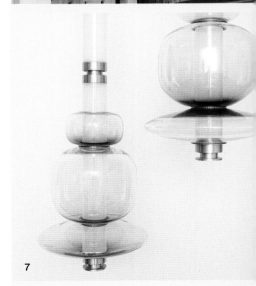

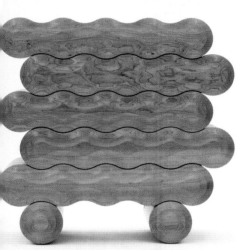

1. Striped yellow partner seats at Grace boutique in Melbourne, a design by Studio Tali Roth.

2. An installation by Alex Proba from Tomorrow Land in Miami's Design District.

3. Colorful MATCH cabinetry by Muller Van Severen for Reform.

4. Apropos Store in Germany designed by Paradowski Studio.

5. Cherry dresser by artist Josh Sperling.

6. Me at The Pridwin Hotel restaurant on Shelter Island, where I fell in love with the Kelly-green booths.

7. Pendant lights from Gabriel Scott's Luna series.

8. Curly Lamp by Stockholm designer Gustaf Westman.

9. Fernando Laposse's Pink Furry Armchair made with agave "hair."

THE PATH UNPLANNED

First things first: To be a good gatherer you have to be a good hunter.

My cardinal rule of style hunting (before we dive into the digital dos and don'ts) is seemingly obvious: Be present. Your surroundings are your first inspiration engine, the fuel that will prompt those online searches later on. Keep your eyes open to architecture that grabs your attention, colors in nature that excite you, details in a restaurant, even the flow as you wander through a hotel lobby.

A few years ago, I was in Florence walking down Via Maggio, in and out of piazzas, when I saw a beautiful inlay pattern on the sidewalk. It stopped me in my tracks — literally! I was so inspired for no particular reason other than it was an incredible work of art. Years later, I used that pattern as inspiration for a client's mosaic bathroom floor. But it could have easily been a rug design or a cool piece of art.

Florence is an obvious portal to inspiration. But these creative snapshots can be found in the most unlikely places. What colors jump out at you when you're walking down your street or driving through your town? Maybe your neighbor has a bed of electric yellow poppies that would be such a cool shade for a front door? Or your local coffee shop painted a checkerboard pattern on their wall, and it has you daydreaming of doing the same to your laundry room floors? My favorite place to look for unexpected color pairings is the grocery store. Don't ever take me to a specialty food market if you're in a hurry, because I will spend an hour in the condiment aisle looking at label designs. The lesson here is stay in tune with what you respond to as you go about your day because inspiration really is everywhere — but you have to be sensitive to it and have a system for keeping track of it.

GO AHEAD AND . . . DO A GOOGLE IMAGE SEARCH

This tool, which is found on Google's homepage, is your best friend when it comes to translating inspirational photos into tangible design. By dragging and dropping your image into the search bar, you're able to do what's called a "reverse search." Meaning, Google will show you like-minded ideas and products you can use in your design projects.

OPPOSITE

I am always returning to the curves architect Richard Meier created at the Getty Center in Los Angeles's Brentwood neighborhood for inspiration. That a structure so solid can also feel so fluid is a total mind-bender.

LET'S GET TO IT

THE PIN PROCESS

On the social battleground, Pinterest is my OG.

Since its inception, I've found this curation tool to be immensely helpful, but here, the specifics matter big time. Keywords are mandatory. The more detailed I make my searches, the better the content being served to me.

If you're looking for living room inspiration, for example, don't just type "modern living rooms." Instead, reference distinct design elements you're drawn to or would like to see together. Maybe something like this: "light blue living rooms with curved sofas, marble mantels, and neon yellow accents." Then, continue to refine from there. Trust me, some really good stuff is about to show up on your boards.

The more you use and interact with this platform, the more in sync your feed will be with your style. So don't simply pin one photo and move on; pay attention to the recommended inspiration that follows. Do any of those images align with your vision? If so, keep pinning. The deeper you go, the more refined the content you are interacting with becomes.

Make sure your pinning includes sources outside of Pinterest, too. It's easy to go down the rabbit hole—I have lost hours of my life in that inspirational abyss—but do a wider search. I love Etsy and a good old-fashioned Google search to start. Other favorites are 1stDibs, Incollect, and The Future Perfect. It helps to download Pinterest's pin button to your browser, which makes it so easy to pin outside images, especially if you use Google Chrome. When you upload from these outlets, Pinterest feeds you like-minded ideas and similar imagery—similar shapes, colors, textures, and even price points. It's another way to communicate what it is you want to see. So, keep your discovery-mode set on overdrive . . . that's really my best advice.

COOL & COLLECTED

Instagram is a bit of a detective game.

Let's put the rumors to rest . . . yes, everything you do on your phone is being tracked. I can't tell you how many times I've told a designer in my studio to research a certain style of lighting or a specific piece of furniture, and the next thing I know, my Instagram is inundated with just that. So, keep looking up what you like; your feed will answer.

My other big recommendation — you could even call it a warning — is to use your search screen wisely. Intention is everything on this platform, and I learned the hard way about being careless with the content I engage with. You know those adorable bunny, kitten, puppy, alpaca, insert-fuzzy-animal-here clips? Well, I thoughtlessly typed "puppies running" in the search bar — and it undid all my carefully curated design prompts. I saw nothing but running puppies in my feed for days, until I eventually liked and interacted with enough design content to undo my moment of weakness.

Don't forget that hashtags are your BFF when it comes to fruitful searches on Instagram. So instead of typing "architecture lover" into your search bar, try "#architecturelover". It may seem like a nominal difference, but a hashtag search will always provide higher caliber, more curated results that go a long way in communicating to the platform what sort of content you want to see.

But I would say the most important thing to remember about Instagram is that you really are creating a community. This point is too often overshadowed by arbitrary likes and the stress of building a mass following. My philosophy has always been to follow people who truly inspire me, engage with them thoughtfully, and show support whenever I can. That's the roadmap that's served me, and I stand by it.

GO AHEAD AND . . . REACH OUT TO THAT INFLUENCER

Don't let a big social following intimidate you. I can't tell you how many makers and artists — with colossal followings — I've reached out to and ended up collaborating with. This is not the moment to simply say hello. But if you have a legitimate question or opportunity, reach out, make the connection — you have nothing to lose and everything to gain. Just hit send!

LET'S TALK CLICKS

We've gotten specific and acknowledged the digital tracking,
but it's the algorithms that really matter.

Pinterest operates on an intricate algorithm cadence. So, click wisely, because each one shapes your journey. The platform tailors itself to your preferences, guiding you down a creative path of your own making. Whatever you do, resist the urge to click aimlessly, and try to be discerning.

If you're serious about tapping more deeply into the Pinterest algorithm, consider upgrading your account to Business, which is free. You get access to more specialized keyword research tools — trends by country, trends by month, trends by year, trends on the rise, and so on.

But the single most effective way to make Pinterest work for you is to use it with consistency. I'm always surprised by how many people tell me they have an account but never use it. Well, that's why their feed isn't showing them anything they want to see. You have to pin. You have to engage. Only then will you crack the code, so to speak, and see everything that makes Pinterest such an amazing tool.

When it comes to Instagram, the algorithm is more of a moving target, continually shifting. Because it's trickier terrain, it demands a

deeper dive — simply using the right keywords and well-defined searches isn't going to cut it here. Getting your feed to give you what you want is a complex cocktail that takes some trial and error to perfect.

Be intentional with who you follow and use your likes wisely. Instagram saves also help capture the attention of the algorithm. Start by focusing on a few key searches at a time, like living rooms and kitchens or neutral spaces and patterned wallpapers. If you take on too many at once, it will take longer for the content you want to see to start showing up in your feed.

So, stick with it and save only what resonates with you. The more you click and follow the winding research path, the richer the content you'll be served. While it takes longer for the experience to tailor itself, compared to Pinterest, eventually a learned aesthetic will take shape in your feed — capturing your musings and turning them into visual gems.

GO AHEAD AND... PAY ATTENTION TO INSTAGRAM'S SUGGESTED FOLLOWS

You know when you follow a new person, and Instagram lines up a row of people and brands it suggests for you based on that follow? Well, take its advice. This is how I found Theo Pinto, the artist who created the painting in my dining room (page 21). His name popped up while I was doing a deep dive into artists. I DMed him — and the rest is, uh, art history.

OPPOSITE

Each of these Soda Square Tables, a design by Yiannis Ghikas for Miniforms, is handblown in Venice, Italy, using Murano glass.

LET'S GET TO IT

CASE OF CATEGORIES

This is where my OCD kicks in.

You could pin or save all the content in the world, but if you don't have a system for easily organizing this inspiration, you'll never find it when you need it. Trust me, I've forfeited hours of my life attempting to retrace my steps to an image. So, as tempting as it is to jump right to the fun stuff (the saving and the pinning), give yourself some time to set up a categorized system of folders for managing what you find. Once you have this intuitive framework in place, the rest will be one seamless motion — find, click, save.

It's taken me years to perfect my network of inspiration folders. After many trials and errors, here's what I've found works best in the design space: On Pinterest, my boards start broad and get increasingly more granular. I'll take a big category like *lighting* and tuck dozens of sub-folders inside: *table lamps, sconces, chandeliers, pendants*, etc. Sometimes, I even go one layer deeper, and divide a subcategory, let's say sconces, by more specific details, like *glass, stone, brass*, and so on.

When it comes to client projects, I work in the same way, but my boards are secret. This is a process game-changer. These secret boards become hubs for curated inspiration organized by room (broad category), and then drilled down to the nitty-gritty details (subcategories). Take the bathroom, for instance. I'll break that down by *stone details, sinks, fixtures, medicine cabinets, toothbrush holders*, you name it. The result is amazing transparency and no detail left unpinned.

Instagram, on the other hand, doesn't play nice with categorized saves, but it's still a gold mine for inspiration. The platform only lets you create overarching folders, which requires a lot more planning on the front end. I tackle this by starting broad, and then breaking out more specific folders as the categories reveal themselves. Here's what I mean by that: If I am looking for furniture with marble detailing, I will create a general *marble furniture* folder, and save everything from consoles to dining tables to whatever else I find and like. But if I notice I'm saving a ton of amazing marble side tables, for example, then I would start a separate folder for those. And that's how one inspiration folder turns into a dozen in a single afternoon.

GO AHEAD AND . . . SAVE EVERYTHING TO PINTEREST

In an ideal world, Instagram would have subcategories that would make filtering and finding related folders easier. But since that's not an option at the moment, I have been known to transfer my Instagram saves to hyper-categorized Pinterest folders. Is it time consuming? Yes. Is it the only way to *really* have everything you need in one place? Unfortunately . . yes.

OPPOSITE
Save with discipline. If there is more than one source of inspiration in a photo, then save it to every folder it pertains to. This Kelly Behun–designed room can be found in my "bathtubs," "seating," and "faucets" folders.

SOURCE CRED

These are the creatives who keep me scrolling and pinning.

THE ARCHITECTS
Elizabeth Roberts
@elizabeth_roberts_architects
Robert Young *@robertyoungarchitects*
Isaac-Rae *@isaac_rae_studio*
Oza Sabbeth *@ozasabbeth*
Workstead *@workstead*

THE CERAMICISTS
Natalie Weinberger
@natalie.weinberger
Jess Murphy *@jessmurphyceramics*
Doppiocotto *@doppiocotto*
Hipnos and Nicte *@hipnosnictehome*
Gergei Erdei *@gergeierdei*

THE CREATIVE COLLECTIVES
Abask *@_abask_*
ClubRoom by Invisible Collection
@clubroombyinvisible
M.A.H Gallery *@mahgallery_london*
The Future Perfect *@thefutureperfect*
Aybar Gallery *@aybargallery*

THE DESIGNERS
Finch Studio *@_finchstudio_*
Chango & Co. *@changoandco*
ALT for Living *@altforliving*
Anthony Authie *@zyvastudio*
Cuff Studio *@cuff_studio*

THE LIGHTING DESIGNERS
Sabine Marcelis *@sabine_marcelis*
Larose Guyon *@larose.guyon*
Roll & Hill *@rollandhill*
The Urban Electric Co.
@urbanelectricco
Farrah Sit *@farrahsit*

THE MULTIDISCIPLINARY ARTISTS
Faye Toogood
@t_o_o_g_o_o_d
Yinka Ilori *@yinka_ilori*
Lisa Hunt *@creativehunt*
Lana Gomez *@lanagomez*
Es Devlin *@esdevlin*

THE PAINTERS
Hannah Polskin *@hannahpolskinstudio*
Theo Pinto *@theopintostudio*
Bradley Theodore *@bradleytheodore*
CJ Hendry *@cj_hendry*
Thomas Gromas *@thomasgromas*

THE PHOTOGRAPHERS
Kerry Wheeler *@worldofkerry*
Jessica Antola *@jessicaantola*
Austin Henry Wallace
@austinhenrywallace
Gentl & Hyers *@gentlandhyers*
Gail Albert Halaban *@gailalberthalaban*

THE SCULPTORS
Annie Morris *@annie_morris_studio*
Samantha Sandbrook
@samanthasandbrook
Whisbe *@whisbe*
Simone Bodmer-Turner
@simonebodmerturner
Henry Baumann *@henry_baumann*

THE SURREALISTS
Santi Zoraidez *@szoraidez*
Andrés Reisinger *@reisingerandres*
Jee Young Lee *@jee_young_lee*
Six N. Five *@sixnfive*
Don Diablo *@dondiablo*

THE TABLETOP MAKERS
Serax *@serax_official*
Henry Holland *@henryhollandstudio*
L'Objet *@lobjet*
Felt+Fat *@feltandfat*
Alexandra Manousakis
@alexandramanousakis

THE TAPESTRY ARTISTS
Lauren Williams *@laurenwilliamsart*
Vanessa Barragão
@vanessabarragao_work
Cindy Hsu Zell *@cindyhsuzell*
Crossing Threads *@crossingthreads*
Jo Elbourne *@j.elbourne*

LET'S GET TO IT

1. Faye Toogood's Fudge Chair.
2. Pistachio dreamscape by Six N. Five.
3. Annie Morris's Stack series.
4. Sabine Marcelis's Totem collection.
5. Balance by Vanessa Barragão.
6. "Butts Up" box by Haas Brothers at L'Objet.
7. Cuff Studio's Arc dining chairs.
8. Stoneware sculpture by Jess Murphy Ceramics.
9. Coupes at ClubRoom by Invisible Collection.

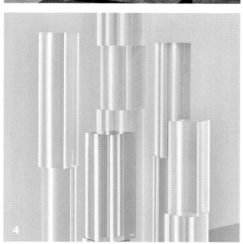

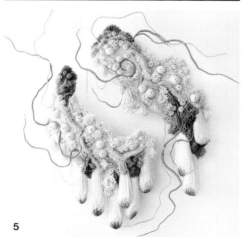

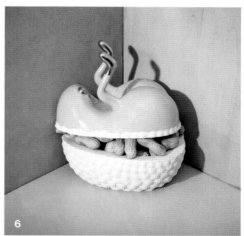

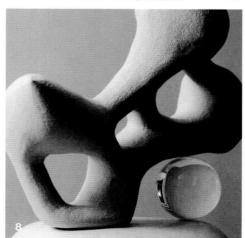

THE VIBE GUIDE

For all the woo-woo lovers out there.

Pinning or hearting a room that caught your eye is one thing. Creating that same mood in your own home . . . not as easy as it looks. There isn't a go-to recipe for making a space *feel* a certain way. But I do have tools I turn to again and again. Elements that, when used together, make design a sensory experience, one that connects as much with the eye as it does with your sense of smell and your spirit.

Specific crystals, colors, and scents can channel a certain vibe-y sensibility. Some inspire creativity or make you feel more grounded. Others invigorate your morning or promote a restful night's sleep. The mere presence of one of these elements is not foolproof, of course. But think of it almost like setting an intention for your space, deciding what it is you need from that room, then acknowledging that decision by investing in one of these elements that promotes it.

Now whether this is mysticism at work or simply a visual reminder to realign your own energy is a question I'll let you answer for yourself. But let me just say, there is a reason my front door is flanked by two massive, negativity-deflecting amethysts (see page 8 for reference).

For a deeper dive into the magic of these mood enhancers, I tapped a few expert friends to help demystify their sensory spirit — and help me help *you* set the right tone at home.

Daydream-inducing moments spent in nature, indelible travels, or perhaps cultural nostalgia — whatever the culprit, scents have the power to bring environments to life. Quick physiology lesson: Our olfactory system, which is responsible for our sense of smell, is closely linked to the brain's limbic system, the part that governs our emotions and memories. It's this connection that makes scent such a powerful tool, especially when you consider it through the lens of interior design.

Scent has the ability, on an unconscious level, to connect us to moments, to places, to people that we love. Introducing a candle that smells like rosemary and warm sunshine, for instance, can cause memories of your summer in Tuscany to bubble up — even if you're standing in your bedroom in Ohio. On a deeper level, certain smells can conjure feelings, like comfort, romance, tranquility, and so on. I spoke with Julien Gommichon, the US president of Diptyque, about the unsung powers of these super scents, and he took me on a deep dive into what makes specific profiles so captivating. Flip the page to learn more.

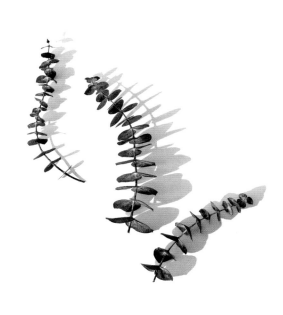

CITRUS

Think lemon, orange, and grapefruit—citrus scents provide a burst of bright energy. Their invigorating nature can improve focus and seriously lift the spirits. Interesting fact: The body experiences a release in serotonin when citrus scents are present.

CORIANDER

The seeds from this flowering herb were used as an aphrodisiac in ancient Greece. Its blossom is considered a symbol of lust. So it is not at all surprising that its scent—a spicy, woodsy, peppery mix—is thought to ignite passion.

EUCALYPTUS

Known as a cure-all for mental and physical fatigue, this scent makes an appearance in many spa-like environments for that very reason. Its menthol-like qualities promote relaxation and wellness—and physically, eucalyptus makes an excellent decongestant.

JASMINE

The sweet, honeyed scent is best known for generating romantic energy. It can also be very effective at improving mood and increasing energy levels. The floral-forward notes promote relaxation and a positive mindset.

LAVENDER

Long revered for its calming and soothing abilities, lavender can help to counter mood, exhaustion, and stress thanks to its ability to calm the nervous system. If your goal is a relaxed atmosphere, this scent is key.

PATCHOULI

You'd be surprised to know just how many fragrances have this warm, earthy note in their ingredient mix. That's because it has such a comforting vibe, which aligns with the belief that it can connect us to nature and our memories.

PEPPERMINT

Famously, this scent is known to alleviate headaches caused by nervous tension. The cooling vapors relieve tight muscles and promote a more restful sleep, too. But it can also be used to invigorate your senses — so really, you can't go wrong here.

PINE

Balmy, earthy, and aromatic — apart from its connection to the holidays, this woodsy scent is exception-ally refreshing and uplifting, and it promotes a boost in positive emotions.

ROSE

For many, the scent of rose evokes feelings of comfort and love. Similar to lavender, though, it is actually excellent for quieting the mind, easing anxieties, and boosting feelings of optimism and hope.

SANDALWOOD

This deep, woody, and often sweet scent is incredibly grounding. It promotes a strong sense of peace and was used during ancient times as a means of spiritual connection and communication. Many cultures believe it can ease the soul.

SCENTS: MORE POWERFUL WHEN PAIRED

Just as specific scents conjure certain moods, it turns out specific combinations can do the same. Our expert, Julien Gommichon of Diptyque, walked me through some of his most influential mixes for when he really wants to stimulate the olfactory receptor.

THE VIBE: INVIGORATED & UPLIFTED

Lavender
Pine
Citrus
Peppermint
Eucalyptus

THE VIBE: SENSUAL & PLAYFUL

Rose
Jasmine

THE VIBE: EMPOWERED & GROUNDED

Coriander
Sandalwood

Color is something, on a surface level, most people consider to be simple and straightforward. Red is red. Blue is blue. Purple is a combination of the two, if you really want to get into it. But dig a little deeper, and you realize it is so much more personal than that. If I say blue, one person could picture cerulean, another navy, another teal, and on it goes.

It's in these delicate nuances of the spectrum that we discover a color's distinct influence on how we feel in — and interact with — a space. No one understands the science behind these happy hues and decadent tones more than Joa Studholme, Farrow & Ball's own color curator. On the next page, she helps me delve into the subtle distinctions from one color to the next, and what their impact is on our psyche.

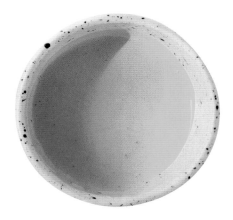

AQUA

Reminiscent of the ocean, it combines the calming qualities of blue with the refreshing and invigorating attributes of green, evoking a sense of clarity, harmony, and emotional balance. A room this color is the perfect spot to give yourself a mental reset.

BLACK

Darks are undeniably moody, but they have a modern slant, too. Deep, rich shades can be soothing and romantic in bedrooms. The hall in Joa Studholme's house has been painted in Farrow & Ball's Down Pipe for fifteen years. The lead gray color's enduring appeal comes from the sense of drama it provides, making sure your first impression is a lasting one.

BLUE

Blue tends to divide opinions more than any other color. For some, it conjures cold, unfriendly spaces, while in others, it evokes a sense of calm and serenity. You know where you land. In any case, blue reflects soothing tones of the sea and the sky, creating rooms with timeless appeal. Farrow & Ball's most relaxed and easy-to-use blues are those that lean towards gray, like Pigeon or Cromarty.

CHARTREUSE

Often associated with energy, vitality, and freshness, this yellow-ish, green-ish, bright-ish hue can inspire creativity, stimulate the mind, and add a lively and uplifting vibe. It's a strong color, so use it sparingly. A little pop around your space will feel unexpected and cool.

GOLD

A warm and radiant color associated with wealth, luxury, and abundance. Often overlooked as a wall color, it conjures feelings of opulence, success, and positivity. Consider it when trying to add a touch of glamour or richness to your space.

GREEN

Green, so often associated with health and good luck, is lush and uplifting. It connects us with nature and promotes a sense of well-being. Use colors you can see from your window frame – the deep shades of the forest or pale hues of a field – to invite the outdoors in. This works wonders, I promise.

LAVENDER

Combining the femininity of pink with the sophistication of gray, this soft shade is known for evoking feelings of nostalgia, subtlety, and elegance. Farrow & Ball's Brassica has warm, rich lavender tones that lift cold-feeling rooms and provide a colorful alternative to slate.

PINK

In the long, dark days of winter, we pine for colors that are uplifting but still mellow. Colors that make us feel like our home is our sanctuary. Studholme loves Sulking Room Pink for this, a tone that is not overtly pink and has a dusky, warm note. Wrap your whole room in this shade—ceiling included—for the ultimate restful retreat.

WHITE

The color of certainty, of illumination, of insight. The sheer magnitude of white hues you can choose from can be overwhelming, but don't let the paint swatch wall get the best of you. There is a shade to work with most any mood, whether you want a subtle, muted feel or a fresh, graphic scheme. Just pay particular attention to the underlying tones—be it warm, stony, or cool.

YELLOW

Rich yellows are often perceived as sunshine, particularly in hallways, where they create a welcoming atmosphere that has both depth and softness. It's impossible not to feel happy in a space covered in Ciara Yellow paint, or cheerful sitting in the warmth of a north-facing room covered in Babouche.

COLORS: A CHEAT SHEET TO ENHANCING YOUR MOOD

Is picking a shade of paint tricky? Yes. Do too many people let it seriously stress them out? Also, yes. Remember, it's just paint. If you get stuck, it helps to stop considering actual colors and instead start thinking in terms of mood. How do you want your room to feel? Answer that question, and then only look at colors which promote that mood.

THE VIBE: CALM & RELAXED

Pale blues
Earthy greens
Nude
Creamy beige
White

THE VIBE: ENERGETIC & INSPIRED

Yellow
Sky blue
Grassy greens
Burnt orange
Turquoise

THE VIBE: MOODY & DRAMATIC

Black
Saturated jewel tones
Deep grays
Almost-black shades
Gold

Healers. Grounders. Power possessors.

Crystals are a thing of beauty, but their superpowers run so much deeper than aesthetic attraction. I like to think of them as little time capsules of knowledge. Consider this: Some of these gemstones were forged during the earliest part of Earth's formation. Just imagine all they experienced during their creation. Scientifically speaking, crystals are structured in a way that makes them able to turn electrical energy into mechanical energy. They can emit certain vibratory frequencies based on the energies around them. This is why you find them in all sorts of technologies.

It's this idea, how the vibratory frequencies of crystals interact with the body, that guides the work of my friend and energy guru Rashia Bell of The Cristalline. She advises clients how to create balanced energy within themselves and their spaces by pairing them with particular crystals, sort of like how a doctor would give you a prescription. There is no one-size-fits-all approach to this sort of healing; however, Bell broke down her favorite stones and their superpowers for us on the following page, crystals that promote everything from health to connectivity.

AMAZONITE

Known as "the gambler's stone," the blue-ish green mineral encourages good luck and fortune. It brings peaceful energy to our interactions with others so that we can express our personal truths without fear while simultaneously maintaining our internal boundaries.

AMETHYST

Commonly used to access the third eye chakra — center of the forehead — and one's intuition, this gemstone's most unique superpower is that it can be used for both energetic protection *and* inner connectivity. In its protection role, it clears the energy of bad influences and attachments. In its connector role, amethyst allows the higher mind to tap into one's true inner self.

BLACK TOURMALINE

A grounding stone that connects us to Earth, black tourmaline eliminates toxic emotions and clears negative thinking — which makes it especially useful if you notice anxiety creeping in. A favorite of both Marie Curie and Nicola Tesla for its ability to generate an electric charge, Rashia Bell of The Cristalline uses hers to protect against electromagnetic stressors.

CARNELIAN

Able to enhance vitality, motivation, and courage, this stone aligns with the sacrum (i.e., your lower pelvis). It resonates with both feminine and masculine energies — and how the two are balanced within each of us. It is an especially powerful companion for women during their monthly cycle and for those having reproductive issues.

CITRINE

An action-oriented stone of manifestation and abundance, it has long been associated with creativity and wealth. But what Bell loves most is its ability to help people stand firmly in their personal power, to limit self-doubt, and establish boundaries in every aspect of their life.

CLEAR QUARTZ

Probably the most commonly recognized crystal of all, this stone is found in a number of countries around the world and has so many uses. Its main properties are to amplify, program, and retain energy in a way that works similarly to muscle memory. It can also align with any area of the body — so if you could only choose one stone to have, this would be it.

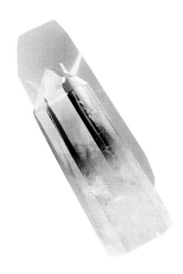

HEMATITE

Helping create balance between the mind and body while aiding in meditation and sleep, it has a grounding energy rooted in attraction, which means it draws positive energy and abundance towards you. That is why Bell loves to use it in manifestation, which is the act of embodying positive intentions into existence in reality.

LABRADORITE

This stone represents wind — an earth element that we can feel and know exists, but can't see or touch. It's beautiful to work with on journeys of self-discovery, and its protective nature supports us, revealing our true path and honoring our destiny.

LAPIS LAZULI

A stone that aligns with your fifth chakra (the throat) and helps alleviate fear and elevate memory and intellect. Bell uses it to channel her ability to speak her truth with grace, ease, and confidence. It's also very useful in energy-draining situations.

MOONSTONE

Associated with intuition, this is a stone of harmony. Its energy is intensely feminine and connected to cycles of reproduction, birth, and, subsequently, rebirth and renewal. Moonstone is also intimately linked to one's inner journey and the mystery of self-discovery, making it beautiful to sit with on full and new moons.

ROSE QUARTZ

Soothing and compassionate, this stone is all about self-care and self-love. It helps calm the mind and body while supporting the heart and the heart chakra. It reminds us that love can heal so many things in our life, and that it all starts with the self.

SELENITE

Known for its cleansing and purifying properties, Bell uses this stone to clear stagnant energy in the body — and the home. Because it vibrates at a very high frequency, this stone can help you connect with your higher self and align with your higher purpose while shielding you from negative outside influences.

SMOKY QUARTZ

This grounding and stabilizing stone is a master at transmuting negativity. It protects one's environment by absorbing toxic energy that needs to be removed. It then transfers that energy into the earth, which grounds and neutralizes it. Bell calls smoky quartz "a compost system for your energetic body."

THE FOLIAGE FILES

Plants, but use them wisely.

Full disclosure: I am not one of those turn-your-house-into-a-jungle plant people. I like them, but in small, thoughtful doses. You won't find me chatting up my succulent while making breakfast. (I have a dog for those conversations.) That said, I don't think a home is complete without houseplants. What they bring to a space — a connection to nature, an organic shape, an unruly touch — is so essential. They are a crucial styling tool.

My rule is, pick your plant and pick your moment. A cascading succulent on a bedside table, herbs on a windowsill, an iconic tree looming over a favorite chair — less is more when it comes to our leafy friends. There is one caveat, of course, and that's care. You may *want* a leafy ficus in your entryway, but will it grow there? Do you know what sort of watering routine you're committing to? Do your homework before making any plant ownership decisions, please.

On that note, here are the plants I turn to most when I want to add a bit of living architecture to a space.

HANGING PLANTS

Graceful vines spilling wildly over a ledge create such a mood. These cascading plants are great when you need to break up sightlines that feel too clean. Suspend one from the ceiling, plant one in a pot, or adhere one to the wall—you won't be disappointed to have a few of these creeping their way through your home.

CRASSULA PELLUCIDA

I love this succulent's heart-shaped leaves—which come in shades of rosy pink, creamy white, and green—and its unruly drape. It's more commonly called Calico Kitten.

MAINTENANCE LOW. **LIGHT** DIRECT SUNLIGHT YEAR-ROUND. **WATER** WHEN SOIL IS FULLY DRY. **SOIL** GOOD DRAINAGE IS KEY—NO WATERLOGGING. **WARNING** TOXIC TO PETS IF INGESTED.

CLEISTOCACTUS COLADEMONONIS

Also known as Monkey Tail, this fast-growing lithophyte cactus has soft, curling stems in white-gingery hues.

MAINTENANCE LOW. **LIGHT** BRIGHT, DIRECT SUNLIGHT YEAR-ROUND. **TIP** PLACE IN A SOUTH- OR WEST-FACING WINDOW. **WATER** EVERY TWO TO THREE WEEKS TO ALLOW SOIL TO FULLY DRY OUT. **WARNING** TOXIC TO PETS IF INGESTED.

COTYLEDON PENDENS

Native to South Africa, this trailing succulent is loved for its bell-shaped flowers and unique fragrance, a blend of lemons and honey.

MAINTENANCE LOW. **LIGHT** BRIGHT, INDIRECT SUNLIGHT. **WATER** DRENCH THOROUGHLY, THEN ALLOW THE TOP INCH OF SOIL TO DRY OUT BEFORE REPEATING. **WARNING** TOXIC TO PETS IF INGESTED.

CRASSULA MARNIERIANA

Architectural by nature, this hard-to-kill plant is commonly referred to as Jade Necklace because of its distinct, vertically stacked leaves etched in pink.

MAINTENANCE LOW. LIGHT BRIGHT, INDIRECT NATURAL LIGHT. SOIL SANDY AND WELL-DRAINED. WATER EVERY ONE TO TWO WEEKS TO ALLOW SOIL TO DRY OUT. PERK PET-FRIENDLY.

SEDUM MORGANIANUM

Affectionately referred to as Burro's Tail, this succulent has cascading, grape-like leaves.

MAINTENANCE LOW. LIGHT PREFERS WARM SUNLIGHT BUT CAN TOLERATE SPURTS OF SHADINESS. WATER EVERY ONE TO TWO WEEKS TO ALLOW SOIL TO DRY OUT. PERK PET-FRIENDLY.

CURIO ROWLEYANUS

A widely adored vining succulent with tiny, pea-shaped leaves, String of Pearls has trailing stems that are robust and fast-growing.

MAINTENANCE LOW. LIGHT HAPPIEST WITH AT LEAST SIX HOURS OF BRIGHT, INDIRECT SUNLIGHT A DAY. WATER EVERY ONE TO TWO WEEKS TO ALLOW SOIL TO DRY OUT. WARNING TOXIC TO PETS IF INGESTED.

HERBS

The aromatic celebs of the kitchen. Who doesn't love an array of freshly potted herbs? But your personal spice squad is not there to simply bring big flavors to your next dish. They can also create petite, fragrant gardens on your countertops and windowsills. This might be the sole exception to my less-is-more credo, because here, I prefer dramatic groupings that add some high-impact sensory magic.

BASIL

Fast-growing and sweet-smelling, its bright green leaves have an appealing pucker to them.

MAINTENANCE MODERATE.
LIGHT A SUN-LOVER WHO PREFERS SOUTH-FACING WINDOWS. **WATER** REGULARLY TO KEEP SOIL MOIST.
PERK PET-FRIENDLY AND AROMATIC.

MINT

The versatile perennial, with its luscious, square-stemmed greenery, brings instant freshness to a room. Fair warning: Its presence has been known to cause strong cravings for sweet tea or mint juleps (at least at my house).

MAINTENANCE MODERATE. **LIGHT** ONLY PARTIAL SUN FOR THIS SHADE LOVER. **SOIL** GOOD DRAINAGE IS KEY – NO WATERLOGGING. **WATER** REGULARLY TO KEEP SOIL LIGHTLY MOIST. **PERK** PET-FRIENDLY AND AROMATIC.

ROSEMARY

Featuring gray-green, needle-like foliage, it releases a strong aroma often associated with cozy vibes and autumn days.

MAINTENANCE MODERATE. **LIGHT** PREFERS SIX HOURS OF FULL SUNLIGHT PER DAY. **SOIL** SANDY WITH GOOD DRAINAGE. **WATER** ONLY WHEN SOIL IS DRY. **PERK** PET-FRIENDLY AND AROMATIC.

SAGE

Cherished for its pungent, soft-to-the-touch leaves, this mint family friend is native to the Mediterranean region, which means it loves to take in some serious sun.

MAINTENANCE MODERATE. LIGHT SIX HOURS OF FULL SUN PER DAY. SOIL SANDY SOIL WITH GOOD DRAINAGE. WATER REGULARLY TO KEEP SOIL EVENLY MOIST, NEVER SOGGY. PERK PET-FRIENDLY AND AROMATIC.

THAI BASIL

With its purple stalks and slender, serrated leaves, this fancy herb has become a bit of a trendsetter with a sweet anise-like fragrance and a subtle spiciness.

MAINTENANCE MODERATE. LIGHT A SUN-LOVER WHO PREFERS SOUTH-FACING WINDOWS. WATER REGULARLY TO KEEP SOIL MOIST. PERK PET-FRIENDLY AND AROMATIC.

THYME

Often wild and unruly, this short-leafed plant is not only a culinary VIP, it also brings a sprawling bushiness to your herbal mix.

MAINTENANCE LOW. LIGHT SIX-TO-EIGHT HOURS OF FULL SUN. WATER ONLY WHEN SOIL IS DRY. PERK PET-FRIENDLY AND AROMATIC.

TREES

Tricky to place. Tricky to care for. Trees can be just plain tricky. So give it some serious thought before bringing a high-maintenance branchy friend home. I like to think of them as organic sculptures that take the place of art. Pick your spot first, and take note of the natural light in that area. Then, this is so important: Only shop for trees that can thrive there. If the tree you want doesn't vibe with the location you chose, just don't do it.

BIRD OF PARADISE

You can spot this plant by its distinctive split leaves. The humidity-lover is named for its orange-blue flowers that resemble a tropical bird – though, sadly, it's rare for one to bloom indoors.

MAINTENANCE MODERATE. **LIGHT** FULL TO PARTIAL SUNLIGHT. **WATER** EVERY ONE TO TWO WEEKS OR WHEN SOIL IS DRY. PREFERS FILTERED WATER TO TAP. **TIP** THE MORE HUMIDITY THE BETTER. **WARNING** TOXIC TO PETS IF INGESTED.

EUCALYPTUS TREE

This tree not only emits a fresh, woody aroma, but its silvery leaves have been revered for their medicinal powers for centuries.

MAINTENANCE MODERATE. **LIGHT** LOVES FULL SUN. AVOID EXPOSURE TO THE COLD. **WATER** DROUGHT TOLERANT. ONLY WATER WHEN SOIL IS DRY. **WARNING** HARMFUL TO PEOPLE AND PETS IF INGESTED.

FICUS BONSAI

Also called a *Ficus microcarpa*, this elegant and calming shrub has twisting, sculptural branches that make a serious architectural statement.

MAINTENANCE MODERATE. **LIGHT** SUN-DRENCHED CONDITIONS ARE BEST. **WATER** LIGHTLY, EVERY FEW DAYS WHEN THE TOP OF SOIL IS DRY. **TIP** AVOID LETTING ROOTS SIT IN WATER. **WARNING** TOXIC TO PETS IF INGESTED.

FIDDLE LEAF FIG

Glossy, violin-shaped leaves and a height that can soar to 10 feet have made this the "It" tree of the moment.

MAINTENANCE MODERATE.
LIGHT BRIGHT INDIRECT LIGHT TO FULL SUN. CAN BENEFIT FROM A FEW HOURS OF DIRECT SUN. WATER EVERY ONE TO TWO WEEKS OR WHEN SOIL IS DRY. WARNING TOXIC TO PETS IF INGESTED.

OLIVE TREE

With small, silvery, gray-green leaves, this Mediterranean native has become a go-to, eye-catching houseplant.

MAINTENANCE HIGH. LIGHT BRIGHT TO FULL SUN. SOUTH AND WEST FACING WINDOWS ARE BEST. CONSIDER GROW LIGHTS IN FALL/WINTER. WATER ONCE A WEEK, WHEN SOIL IS DRIED HALFWAY DOWN THE ROOTS. TOLERATES NORMAL ROOM HUMIDITY LEVELS. PERK PET-FRIENDLY.

YUCCA GIGANTEA

A mess of spiky, sword-like leaves shoot from the top of a stick-straight trunk, making this plant a useful tool when you want to draw the eye up to the ceiling.

MAINTENANCE MODERATE.
LIGHT INDIRECT WITH A FEW HOURS OF DIRECT SUN DAILY.
WATER EVERY ONE TO TWO WEEKS OR WHEN SOIL IS DRY. WARNING TOXIC TO PETS IF INGESTED.

SUCCULENTS

These guys are the low-maintenance rock stars of the plant kingdom. With their laid-back charm and easygoing nature, they turn nooks and crannies into lush still-life displays. I love to play around with the small varieties. Their petite stature isn't to be underestimated. What they lack in size, they make up for in statement-making details. Think alien-like forms and bulbous, water-filled leaves.

ALOE VERA

With its distinctive lance-shaped leaves and a checklist of dermatologist-approved benefits, this air purifier is so hardy it could thrive in even the driest conditions.

MAINTENANCE LOW.
LIGHT LOVES FULL TO PARTIAL SUNLIGHT. **WATER** EVERY TWO TO THREE WEEKS WHEN SOIL IS DRY.
WARNING TOXIC TO PETS IF INGESTED.

CRASSULA CANDY CANE

A shrublet with long, finger-like leaves, this plant has color-changing talents that make it truly special. In full sun, the usually white and mint green leaves turn a deep, blushing rose.

MAINTENANCE LOW. **LIGHT** FULL SUNLIGHT. **WATER** ONLY WHEN SOIL IS DRY. **PERK** PET-FRIENDLY.

CRASSULA IVORY TOWERS

Also called *Crassula conjuncta*, it has silvery-green leaves that grow in compact rosettes stacked one atop the next giving it a delicate, tentacle-like form.

MAINTENANCE LOW. **LIGHT** FULL SUN. **WATER** ONLY WHEN SOIL IS DRY. **PERK** PET-FRIENDLY.

CRASSULA MOONGLOW

Pretty rare but worth the hunt, it has fleshy, gray-green clusters that form compact square rosettes. The velvety clusters stack to create columns that can reach 18 inches in height.

MAINTENANCE LOW. LIGHT FULL SUNLIGHT. WATER ONLY WHEN SOIL IS DRY. TIP FULLY SATURATE SOIL WHEN YOU DO WATER. PERK PET-FRIENDLY.

ECHEVERIA

These rose-shaped, flowering succulents are fast-growing and come in a stunning array of colors (from pale green to deep purple) and sizes.

MAINTENANCE LOW. LIGHT FULL SUNLIGHT. WATER EVERY TWO TO THREE WEEKS WHEN SOIL IS DRY. PERK PET-FRIENDLY.

TIGER JADE

You can't miss its wildly patterned foliage—dark green or blackish-green spots with vibrant bands.

MAINTENANCE LOW. LIGHT BRIGHT INDIRECT LIGHT. WATER EVERY TWO TO THREE WEEKS WHEN SOIL IS DRY. PERK PET-FRIENDLY.

FLOWERING PLANTS

Getting a plant to bloom consistently indoors is a feat in and of itself. But what those vibrant bursts of color bring to a room makes this somewhat-fussy option worth the effort. Like trees, you have to pay close attention to the care it needs to thrive. As a universal rule for this category, sunlight is the key ingredient. Without enough of it, your flowering plant won't be able to do its thing.

OXALIS TRIANGULARIS

The deep purple, butterfly-like leaves of the False Shamrock close up each night only to spring open again come morning. A little bit of natural magic to look forward to with your coffee.

MAINTENANCE MODERATE.
LIGHT BRIGHT INDIRECT LIGHT WITH A FEW HOURS OF DIRECT MORNING SUN. **SOIL** GRITTY, WELL-DRAINED SOIL. **WATER** SPARINGLY TO MAINTAIN BARELY MOIST SOIL. **FLOWERS** SPRING TO SUMMER. **WARNING** TOXIC TO PETS IF INGESTED.

SUNDEW

A geyser of little red blooms wobbling atop long woody stems, this exotic plant is all drama—and not just because it entraps any bug that happens to land on its sticky pads.

MAINTENANCE MODERATE.
LIGHT A FEW HOURS OF FULL SUN DAILY (OR PLACE NEAR AN ARTIFICIAL LIGHT SOURCE). **WATER** FROM BELOW BY SITTING ITS POT IN A SAUCER FILLED WITH ONE INCH OF SOFT WATER OR RAINWATER. **FLOWERS** LATE SUMMER TO FALL. **PERK** PET-FRIENDLY.

GARDENIA

Skip the scented candle and go straight for the real thing. The sweet (but not too sweet) scent coming from this shrub-like perennial is intoxicating.

MAINTENANCE HIGH. **LIGHT** BRIGHT INDIRECT LIGHT. AVOID DIRECT SUN. **WATER** WEEKLY TO KEEP SOIL CONSISTENTLY DAMP, NOT SOGGY. **FLOWERS** SPRING TO SUMMER. **WARNING** TOXIC TO PETS IF INGESTED.

LAVENDER

Look for dwarf varieties that work best indoors. I like Munstead for its dense clusters of dark purple-blue blooms. You can cut and dry the stems or even add its buds to your baked goods.

MAINTENANCE LOW. **LIGHT** FULL SUN. **SOIL** GRITTY, WELL-DRAINED SOIL. **WATER** DEEPLY EVERY TWO WEEKS. **FLOWERS** SUMMER. **PERK** PET-FRIENDLY.

KAPA-KAPA PLANT

Not your average houseplant, its lush foliage, pink stems, and neon-pink flowers throw a three-to-four month-long floral fiesta. (Always stealing the spotlight, this one.)

MAINTENANCE MODERATE. **LIGHT** INDIRECT SUNLIGHT TO PARTIAL SHADE. **WATER** ONCE A WEEK OR WHEN THE TOP TWO INCHES OF SOIL ARE DRY. PLACE NEAR A HUMIDIFIER IN WINTER. **FLOWERS** SPRING TO SUMMER. **PERK** PET-FRIENDLY.

ORCHIDS

Despite its high-maintenance reputation, there are easy-to-care-for orchids, like the *Dendrobium* varieties, which deliver an impressive display of vibrant blooms.

MAINTENANCE MODERATE. **LIGHT** PARTIAL TO BRIGHT INDIRECT SUNLIGHT. **WATER** EVERY ONE TO TWO WEEKS WHEN SOIL IS DRY. **FLOWERS** LATE WINTER TO EARLY SPRING AND LAST UP TO SIX WEEKS. **PERK** PET-FRIENDLY.

FLOOR PLANTS

Extra-long, extra-big, extra-colorful, extra-full — these guys bring something *extra* to a room. With their commanding stature and tropical vibes, they have a knack for turning any space into a lush oasis. But I think their true superpower is as a styling tool; they add visual layers no inanimate object can replicate. Flanking an entryway or holed up in a corner, everything is always about them — which, if I'm honest, is how it should be.

DRACAENA LEMON LIME

Rocking mottled green leaves with gold variegated edges, this tropical plant is virtually indestructible and doubles as a detox champion, removing harmful toxins from the air around the clock.

MAINTENANCE LOW. **LIGHT** PREFERS MEDIUM TO BRIGHT INDIRECT LIGHT. WILL TOLERATE LOW INDIRECT LIGHT SOMETIMES. **WATER** EVERY TWO TO THREE WEEKS WHEN SOIL IS DRY. **WARNING** MILDLY TOXIC TO DOGS IF INGESTED.

BEGONIA MACULATA

The plant version of a tropical heartthrob, it has asymmetrical, silver-spotted leaves with a touch of claret underneath.

MAINTENANCE MODERATE. **LIGHT** INDIRECT SUNLIGHT. **WATER** EVERY ONE TO TWO WEEKS WHEN SOIL IS DRY. **TIP** PREFERS WARM SPACES. KEEP AWAY FROM HEATING VENTS AND RADIATORS. **WARNING** TOXIC FOR PETS.

BRIGHAMIA INSIGNIS

Also known as Cabbage on a Stick, the Hawaiian palm is sculpturally dramatic.

MAINTENANCE LOW. **LIGHT** BRIGHT INDIRECT LIGHT. **WATER** ONLY WHEN SOIL IS DRY. **TIP** PREFERS WARM SPACES. KEEP AWAY FROM HEATING VENTS AND RADIATORS. **PERK** PET-FRIENDLY.

BEGONIA SPACESTAR MAIA

Like nothing you've ever seen before, its pink-tipped leaves and awesomely odd shape prove you can be low-maintenance and high-style at the same time.

MAINTENANCE LOW. **LIGHT** BRIGHT INDIRECT LIGHT. **WATER** EVERY ONE TO TWO WEEKS WHEN SOIL IS DRY. **PERK** PET-FRIENDLY.

ZAMIOCULCAS ZAMIIFOLIA 'RAVEN'

Stunningly dark, effortlessly chic, and absolutely forgiving (if you happen to have a history of plant neglect).

MAINTENANCE LOW. **LIGHT** BRIGHT INDIRECT LIGHT. **WATER** EVERY TWO TO THREE WEEKS WHEN SOIL IS DRY. **WARNING** TOXIC TO PETS IF INGESTED.

CALATHEA ROSEOPICTA 'MEDALLION'

Large, silver-green leaves with feather-like markings and a purple-pink underside, this is a striking choice if you have an always-warm room with good humidity.

MAINTENANCE LOW. **LIGHT** BRIGHT INDIRECT LIGHT. CAN HANDLE SOME SHADE. **WATER** WEEKLY TO KEEP SOIL CONSISTENTLY DAMP, NOT SOGGY. **PERK** PET-FRIENDLY.

THE IT, IT-LIST

Twenty years of my carefully curated—tried and tested—design sources compiled in one all-encompassing guide. From fabrics to flooring to appliances, this is everyone you need to know before starting your next mini (or massive) makeover.

A Monogram oven in a kitchen I designed in the Hamptons.

APPLIANCES

AGA*
Since 1922, this British brand has captured hearts with its Classic range, celebrated for its heat-retaining, efficient, and recyclable cast-iron design. *agarangeusa.com*

ASKO*
Craftsmanship, style, and water and energy efficiency have taken this company from humble beginnings in a Swedish farming community to a household name. *asko.com*

BOSCH*
With a transparent sustainability report and climate mitigating efforts, these appliances offer incredible quality, bringing efficient and stay-fresh technologies into the heart of your home. *bosch.us*

DACOR
These California-made appliances combine innovative technology and exceptional materials, elevating the art of living well. *dacor.com*

DCS
Established in Huntington Beach, this West Coast open-air kitchen company has passionately embraced the outdoor lifestyle. *dcsappliances.com*

FISHER & PAYKEL
These appliances combine luxury and functionality, with products that have earned Energy Star and WELS (Water Efficiency Labeling and Standards) ratings. *fisherpaykel.com*

GAGGENAU
Rooted in craftsmanship since 1683, every appliance bears the mark of exceptional design and performance—evident in their partnership with chefs from Michelin-starred restaurants. *gaggenau.com*

JENNAIR
Pushing boundaries in technology, finishes, and materials (think laser-etched lace and mixed metals), this appliance and ventilation force challenges norms with industry-first exclusives. *jennair.com*

LA CORNUE
Maintaining its artistic traditions since 1908, the iconic Parisian range is handcrafted by specialists in steel, copper, and brass in a rainbow of colorways. *lacornueusa.com*

LYNX
A team of restaurant industry pros brought their expertise to the outdoor cooking experience, combining elegance with proprietary engineering know-how. *lynxgrills.com*

MIELE*
This appliance titan credits its "forever better" mentality to its German craftsmanship and cutting-edge innovation as well as its efforts to improve the planet. *mieleusa.com*

MONOGRAM
Thanks to technological advances like hearth ovens, whose ventilation actually cleans the air, this brand is redefining luxury appliances. *monogram.com*

THERMADOR
With a host of smart technology features, trade benefits, and efforts to further diversity in design, the brand continues to elevate everyday living. *thermador.com*

SMEG*
The retro design of these Italian-made appliances is eye-catching enough, but their use of renewable resources in the production process makes them even more desirable. *smeg.com*

SUB-ZERO, WOLF, AND COVE*
Committed to sustainability, this industry leader in refrigeration, cooking, and dishwashing equipment has mastered environmental preservation, making strides in energy efficiency and waste reduction. *subzero-wolf.com*

VIKING
Built on the principles of southern hospitality thanks to its Mississippi roots, this professional-grade range of appliances turns homes into first-class restaurants. *vikingrange.com*

*A sustainable brand.

**To the trade/available through a designer only.

A piece by Belgian artist Thomas Gromas hangs in my hallway.

CABINETRY

BACZEWSKI LUXURY CABINETS
With a curated selection of styles, wood types, finishes, and hardware, the company works with you to deliver modern European designs for the kitchen, bathroom, and closet.
baczewskiluxury.com

BAKES & KROPP
Using locally sourced domestic hardwoods in their Michigan-based workshop, a team of woodworkers crafts luxury cabinetry so custom that no two kitchens are alike.
bakesandkropp.com

CIUFFO CABINETRY
Old World craftsmanship combines with modern technology to create custom cabinetry and millwork in an array of styles from traditional to contemporary. *ciuffocabinetry.com*

D&T CABINETS
Custom cabinetry solutions for kitchens, vanities, built-ins, closets, and more; they specialize in transforming clients' visions into meticulously crafted reality.
dtcabinetsinc.com

FORM KITCHENS*
Built with renewable and recycled materials, these made-to-order, pre-assembled cabinets are revolutionizing well-designed spaces with modern styles that emphasize a personalized approach.
formkitchens.com

HUDSON CABINETRY DESIGN
Located in Peekskill, New York, this team of artisan woodworkers handcrafts custom kitchen cabinetry, built-ins, and bookcases, balancing aesthetic appeal with functional design.
hudsoncabinetrydesign.com

MOUSER CABINETRY*
Crafting custom, fine-wood cabinetry since 1955, this Kentucky company has been recognized by the Kitchen Cabinet Manufacturers Association for its environmental stewardship.
mousercabinetry.com

REFORM*
Offering a new perspective on kitchen design, this Danish brand is where craftsmanship meets a modular framework, and it is made in collaboration with leading architects and designers.
reformcph.com

ART

ARTSTAR
This online platform is curated by market experts who travel the globe to bring exclusive, museum-quality fine art prints by contemporary artists to collectors. *artstar.com*

ARTSY
Armed with art advisors, this marketplace empowers novice and seasoned buyers to follow the art market and global trends as they build their collections. *artsy.net*

DANE FINE ART
Featuring new and established artists from Alexander Calder to Banksy and Basquiat, this gallery ensures transparent transactions and competitive pricing.
danefineart.com

GALERIE BSL
Founded by Béatrice Saint-Laurent, this gallery challenges the boundaries of art and design with functional sculptures that spark the imagination. *galeriebsl.com*

MARTHA STURDY
Materials like brass, bronze, and resin take new shape at the hands of this Vancouver-born conceptual and contemporary sculptor.
marthasturdy.com

HAPI ART
Kristi Kohut's vibrant creations add rays of sunshine to your home, I especially love the embellishments like neon frames. *hapiart.com*

LEFTBANK ART**
In-house artists and a global list of collaborators create handcrafted multimedia artworks for every type of setting. *leftbankart.com*

OLIVER GAL
Founded by sisters Ana Sánchez-Gal and Lola Sánchez, this fashionable South Florida lifestyle studio creates original, hand-embellished art that captures life's haute moments. *olivergal.com*

SAATCHI ART
Turn to this curated online gallery for diverse artistic expressions and guidance on acquiring exceptional pieces from talented emerging artists worldwide. *saatchiart.com*

BASIS cabinetry by Reform.

CRYSTALS

ASTRO GALLERY
One of the world's most established gem and mineral galleries, they carry rare, museum-quality specimens that are truly special. *astrogallery.com*

CRYSTAL AGE
This crystal emporium gives you all the guidance needed to understand minerals, stones, and their connection to your chakras through the use of pendants, beads, fossils, healing stones, and more. *crystalage.com*

CRYSTALS.COM
This curated collection includes hand-selected crystals sourced from around the world for their healing, guiding, protective, and enhancing properties. *crystals.com*

CRYSTALS & STONES
Monthly crystal subscription boxes, energy stone kits, and a selection of essential oils that act as energy tools designed to enhance spirituality and emotional well-being, this Miami-based retailer offers so many ways to interact. *crystalsandstones.com*

ENERGY MUSE
Crystal energy, ancient Chinese symbolism, and numerology come together in this line of intentional, transformative jewelry and gems. *energymuse.com*

PACIFIC MINERALS
This family-owned retailer only deals in ethically sourced stones. Check in often; their large selection is updated daily. *pacificminerals.shop*

PHILLIPS COLLECTION*
Run by founding members of the Sustainable Furnishings Council, this brand celebrates the treasures beneath Earth's surface with its Elements collection of semi-precious stones. *phillipscollection.com*

ROCK PARADISE
This team of gem experts travels to mines around the world searching for high-quality crystals to bring back to Los Angeles. *rockparadise.com*

RON DIER DESIGN
A mineral enthusiast, this West Coast sculptor and furniture designer is known for incorporating impressively large specimens (amethyst, onyx, selenite) into his functional creations. *rondierdesign.com*

SAGE CRYSTALS
All-natural, ethically sourced gemstones charged with Reiki energy to promote self-love, healing, and the power of intuition from a woman-owned haven in Oregon. *sagecrystals.com*

Haas Brothers "Disco Lynda Box" at L'Objet.

A large agnitite specimen.

DECORATIVE ACCENTS

ABASK
This curated selection of globally sourced, collectible objects-turned-modern heirlooms celebrates the skills of artisans and contemporary craftspeople. *abask.com*

ANN SANDRA
The mother-daughter team behind this Bethesda, Maryland, boutique has the most wonderful way of mixing legacy brands with modern favorites. The edit is always spot-on. *annsandra.com*

CURRENT HOME
A New York institution with a little bit of everything: tabletop, seasonal finds, decorative objects, and more. *currenthomeny.com*

LAM CERAMICA
Michele Hickey Gemin brings her minimalist, sculptural designs to Venice, Italy, where her studio showcases her fusion of wheel-throwing and hand-building techniques. *lamvenezia.com*

L'OBJET
The whimsical and slightly cheeky world of founder and creative director Elad Yifrach is bursting with gorgeously eclectic design objects — some designed by him, some by makers met during his global travels. *l-objet.com*

MAISONGAMES
Backgammon, chess, and tic-tac-toe get an artisanal makeover thanks to these acrylic boards and game pieces that bring the imagination to life. *maisongames.com*

SALVATORI
Known for its matte-finished marble fittings and furniture, this brand also creates a line of understated-yet-iconic stone objects made in Italy. *salvatoriofficial.com*

UAUPROJECT*
Based in Warsaw, Poland, this design studio creates 3D-printed home accessories using plant-based bioplastics that are compostable and recyclable. *uauproject.com*

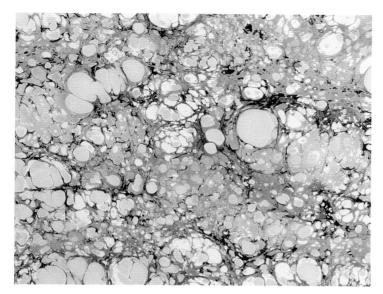

Topo Fabric at Rule of Three.

FABRICS

AIMÉE WILDER
Bespoke hand-printed and digital pigment-printed fabrics and wallpapers presented in a vibrant array of colors and patterns. *aimeewilder.com*

ALT FOR LIVING
Analisse Taft-Gersten has redefined luxury in the fabric world with her innovative one-stop-shop experience, which turned her showrooms into immersive environments. *altforliving.com*

ANTHONY GEORGE HOME
Inspired by travel, each fabric tells a rich story of culture, tradition, and history that imparts soul and spirit into a space.
anthonygeorgehome.com

ARABEL FABRICS
A brand committed to high-quality goods, swift deliveries, and personalized service, all while elevating the fabric experience. *arabelfabrics.com*

BRADLEY
You'll find innovative luxury fabrics from creative design brands with an exclusive collection of linens, silks, and velvets. *bradleyusa.com*

BROOK PERDIGON TEXTILES*
A fabric house that blends historical techniques with modern methods, they transform Belgian linen into unique textiles and digitally printed wallpapers on vellum or grasscloth. *brookperdigontextiles.com*

C&C MILANO
Their exquisite textiles, crafted from precious natural fibers (cashmere, linen, silk, and velvet), create a harmonious fusion of warm and vibrant patterns. *cec-milano.us*

CAROLINE CECIL
An artistic trailblazer transforming ink paintings into ethereal coastal-inspired textiles, wallpapers, and pillows. *carolinececiltextiles.com*

CAROLINE Z HURLEY*
Rooted in creativity and mindful living, their hand-printed, block-printed, and silk-screened fabrics embody the artist's belief that a thoughtfully designed space fosters a sense of calm and connection. *carolinezhurley.com*

CASTEL
A luxury textile brand sourcing the highest-quality fabrics from skilled artisans around the globe. *castelmaison.com*

CHRISTOPHER FARR
Each collection showcases a harmonious blend of historical and contemporary influences, with hand- and screen-printed designs produced at a family-owned, UK-based printer. *christopherfarrcloth.com*

CLAREMONT
Known for its specialized archive sourced from small, European textile manufacturers, the company's distinct fabrics, woven on old looms, are favored by top designers for their timeless quality. *claremontfurnishing.com*

CLARENCE HOUSE
Famous for its vibrant screen-printed fabrics and hand-loomed brocades, the New York–based studio also dabbles in luxurious silks, soft cottons, and rich leathers. *clarencehouse.com*

CORAGGIO
With more than forty years of experience, the brand curates a collection of the world's finest textiles, delicately balancing contemporary aesthetics and a luxurious hand-feel. *coraggio.com*

CW STOCKWELL
With an exquisite blend of heritage and innovation, this West Coast brand boasts an exclusive selection of hand-printed linens and woven performance fabrics. *cwstockwell.com*

DEDAR
An esteemed, family-run design house out of Italy. Their creations blend cutting-edge design with the rich heritage of textile art, telling an ancient tale through intricate woven details, yarns, and colors. *dedar.com*

DONGHIA
Founded by Angelo Donghia in the 1960s, the collection is inspired by art, architecture, fashion, and heritage – offering a blend of luxury and durability. *kravet.com/donghia*

ELWORTHY STUDIO*
Their digitally printed designs not only capture intricate details and textures, but also reflect an eco-conscious ethos, minimizing waste and preserving the essence of each artistic creation. *elworthystudio.com*

ELLISHA ALEXINA
This Boston brand unites exquisite aesthetics with meticulous craftsmanship while reflecting the founder's passion for heritage and global connections. *ellishaalexina.com*

ESKAYEL*
Drawing inspiration from breathtaking landscapes, the Brooklyn-based studio transforms original paintings into dreamy textile creations using inks made from water-based pigments. *eskayel.com*

EUNICE PARK TEXTILES*
Operating on a made-to-order basis, they produce only what is needed, embracing a sustainable approach to creativity. *euniceparktextiles.com*

EVA SONAIKE
The prominent London-based interiors brand weaves an elegant West-African aesthetic into their luxury home textiles and soft furnishings. *evasonaike.com*

FABRIC & STEEL*
Using fabrics crafted in Europe and hand-screen printed in New England, they create architectural elements that embody a perfect blend of permanence and fleeting beauty. *fabricandsteel.com*

FISHMAN'S FABRICS
With a rich heritage dating back to 1903, this brand continues its legacy of sourcing and trading beautiful fabrics from the world's premier mills. *fishmansfabrics.com*

FLOCK
Under the guidance of creative director Jenny Wingfield, this British studio collaborates with artists and recent graduates to curate a vibrant collection of textiles. *flock.org.uk*

FORTUNY
Timeless textiles produced in the same Venetian factory as those created by its renowned founder, Mariano Fortuny, more than a century ago. *fortuny.com*

GASTÓN Y DANIELA
With a legacy spanning more than 130 years, the Spanish design house is known for utilizing the finest materials and luxury craftsmanship to create timeless designs. *gastonydaniela.com*

GREIGE TEXTILES
Linen from Belgium. Artistry from California. Greige presents a captivating blend of durability and beauty. *greigetextiles.com*

HARBINGER
A multi-line showroom founded by designer Joe Lucas, who curates an exceptional blend of globally sourced textile treasures. *harbingerla.com*

HOLLAND & SHERRY
Setting the standard for quality and craft, the nearly two-hundred-year-old mill marries traditional apparel fabrics with innovative interior design, resulting in a diverse range of products. *hollandandsherry.com*

HOLLY HUNT
These fabrics represent the epitome of luxury and performance, offering a beautiful selection that includes exquisite linens, alpacas, cashmeres, and silks. *hollyhunt.com*

IMOGEN HEATH
With an instinctive and experimental approach, Heath draws inspiration from nature and architecture when producing her handcrafted textiles in the UK. *imogenheath.com*

ISOBEL
Inspired by her background in ceramics, Isobel Mills brings a unique perspective to her fabric designs, fusing a love for malleable materials with a playful approach to shape and scale. *shopisobel.com*

JAMES DUNLOP TEXTILES
With a rich heritage dating back to 1907 in Dunedin, New Zealand, the brand embodies a unique perspective on fabric that's grounded in their Australasian identity. *jamesdunloptextiles.com*

JIUN HO
A passionate designer and world traveler, his curated textile collection, a result of his own photography and collaborations with skilled mills around the world, tells captivating stories in fabrics from linen to satin. *jiunho.com*

KATE LOUDOUN SHAND*
Through archival research, the team creates sustainable, rich, and modern fabrics that cater to the curious and imaginative. *kateloudounshand.com*

KERRI ROSENTHAL
With more than two hundred fabrics and wallpapers, Kerri's designs, marked by her iconic Drippy Heart series, bring instant joy and infectious energy to a space. *kerrirosenthal.com*

KERRY JOYCE TEXTILES
The renowned interior designer seamlessly translated his artistic vision into textiles with a collection characterized by historical influences, vibrant visuals, and subtle hues. *kerryjoyce.com*

LAINE + ALLIAGE
Based in New York, this design atelier is known for its exquisite, handmade mural wallpapers. But I love their textiles, a highly edited selection that happens to match the wallcoverings. *laine-and-alliage.com*

LEE JOFA
A two-hundred-year-old brand with a thing for iconic floral patterns, I especially love their modern collections by big-name designers like Kelly Wearstler that bring a bolder expression of materiality and color. *kravet.com/lee-jofa*

LINDSAY COWLES
Through large-scale abstract paintings, Cowles explores the interplay of color and texture, then transforms these artworks into customizable patterns for textiles. *lindsaycowles.com*

MÉTAPHORES*
Closely tied to the Hermès textile legacy, this French design house crafts fabrics through a harmonious blend of material, history, and skilled craftsmanship. *metaphores.com*

MITCHELL FABRICS
An industry giant, they stock more than three thousand decorative fabrics catering to every style and budget. *mitchellfabrics.com*

MOLLY MAHON
Based in the heart of the Ashdown Forest in Sussex, England, Molly is known for her charming fabric designs and passion for block printing. *mollymahon.com*

OPUZEN*
What was once a one-woman operation specializing in hand-dyed textiles is today a leading fabric supplier offering everything from digital prints to one-of-a-kind woven upholstery. *opuzen.com*

PAOLA MELENDEZ | CASA*
These fabrics, born from slow production methods and sustainable raw materials, reflect the beauty of nature, art, travel, and vibrant colors. *paolamelendezcasa.com*

PERENNIALS*
Technical fabrics that are fade-, mildew-, and mold-resistant and easily maintained are what they do. *perennialsfabrics.com*

PETER FASANO
This New York–based brand has a legacy spanning four decades. Its fabrics embody timeless patterns and an artisanal quality. *peterfasano.com*

PIERRE FREY
With styles ranging from the traditional to the whimsical, this French design house is known for its patterns and vivid textures, as well as its extensive historical archives, which date back to the sixteenth century. *pierrefrey.com*

POLLACK
The designers at this boutique studio are, first and foremost, weavers. Each studied the architecture of cloth, how to build a fabric from the ground up. *pollackassociates.com*

REBECCA ATWOOD
Inspired by the sensory adventures of her Cape Cod upbringing, she blends artistry and nature in her specialty-dyed warp fabrics. *rebeccaatwood.com*

ROMO
A rich array of solids and prints, from bold botanicals to rustic plaids, by a storied, family-operated, British fabric house. *romo.com*

RUBELLI
Inspired by its rich Venetian heritage, these fabric collections evoke the grandeur of the Palais des Doges, showcasing a tradition of timeless elegance and exquisite craftsmanship. *rubelli.com*

RULE OF THREE
Working with traditional dyeing and ancient marbling techniques, the LA-based brand transforms fine silks, linens, cottons, and leathers in new and unexpected ways. *ruleofthreestudio.com*

S. HARRIS
Blending heritage with innovation, infusing artistic interpretation with striking color palettes, this century-old brand creates timeless fabrics and trims. *fabricut.com/sharris*

SAVANNAH HAYES
Each fabric features brushstroke and inkblot designs that exude an urban, graphic aesthetic. *savannahhayes.com*

SCALAMANDRÉ
Two words: Zebras collection. This iconic print is part of the New York textile giant's ninety-year legacy that blends trend with tradition. *scalamandre.com*

SEEMA KRISH*
In the rich tradition of Indian hand-block printing, each yard of fabric is stamped using beautifully carved teak wood blocks and GOTS certified dyes. *seemakrish.com*

SOMERSELLE
High-end artisanal fabrics sourced from around the world; you'll find unique bouclés and beautiful prints adapted from original artworks. *somerselle.com*

STONE TEXTILE STUDIO
Interior designer Elizabeth Mollen offers a curated collection of textiles that celebrate everyday simplicity. *stonetextilestudio.com*

STUDIO FOUR NYC
This showroom is a global hub for established design leaders and emerging boutiques, housing an eclectic mix of prints, solids, and sheers. *studiofournyc.com*

TAYLOR MURPHY DESIGN
Based in Austin, Texas, this design house creates a handful of abstract, painterly patterns for when you need something out-of-the-box and bold. *taylorwmurphy.com*

TIBOR
Masters of texture, this heritage brand is at the forefront of innovative woven techniques and spins all of its own bespoke yarns in England. *tibor.co.uk*

VENABLE MOORE*
A female-founded, artist-led design studio in LA dedicated to sustainably printed European linen in a handful of colorful prints. *venablemoore.com*

VILLA NOVA
Graphic embroideries are the standout here, though you'll find a complete lineup of versatile basics, from sheers to velvets. *villanova.co.uk*

WEITZNER*
With industry leader Lori Weitzner at the helm, this studio creates in five robust product categories, from an indoor/outdoor lineup to a truly special handmade collection. *weitznerlimited.com*

ZAK + FOX
An assortment that manages to feel all-encompassing without being overwhelming; they champion the artisan-made and traditionally crafted. *zakandfox.com*

ZINC TEXTILE
Taking texture to exaggerated proportions, their extensive lineup includes some of my favorite chunky bouclés and embroidered velvets. *zinctextile.com*

ZOE GLENCROSS
Each of the pretty prints in this collection begins as a hand-sketched pattern that's silk-screened or lino-carved on linen to preserve a grainy, imperfect finish. *zoeglencross.com*

FLOORING

ARCA STUDIO
Their work with cutting-edge technology and design industry leaders makes them *the* place to find rare and truly original materials. *arcaww.com*

CARLISLE WIDE PLANK FLOORS
The name says it all. This fifty-year-old brand produces exquisite wide-plank, American-made hardwood, pine, and reclaimed wood floors. *wideplankflooring.com*

THE HUDSON COMPANY*
Offering a distinct range of hand-finished flooring, this small, Hudson, New York–based mill ensures a collaborative experience rooted in a commitment to quality and local craftsmanship. *thehudsonco.com*

I.J. PEISER'S SONS
Installing exquisite wood floors for more than a century, the NYC-based experts are true parquetry artists, specializing in intricate – and historically accurate – installations of luxury hardwoods. *ijpeiser.com*

MADERA
This bicoastal – NYC and LA – studio works with an edited-but-beautiful selection of species: European Oak, Northern White Oak, Black Walnut, White Ash, and Antique Heart Pine. *maderasurfaces.com*

PID FLOORS
The brand's mantra, "something for everyone," is made all the more accessible thanks to an innovative online tool that allows you to "view" their floors in your space by simply uploading a photo. *pidfloors.com*

STORIA
Their Miami Design District showroom houses a curated selection of hardwood floors, natural stones, and porcelain tiles, reflecting its commitment to crafts-manship and aesthetic diversity. *storiaflooring.com*

WOODWORKS*
Extraordinary handcrafted and finished wood floors made in Britain. Their reclaimed collection is not only stunning but keeps your project carbon neutral. *woodworks1988.com*

Channel Swivel Chair by Cuff Studio.

Ca'Dona oak flooring from Arca.

FURNISHINGS

ANNA KARLIN
The artist's holistic approach to design intertwines various disciplines, resulting in furnishings that act as jewelry for the home. *annakarlin.com*

ARTERIORS*
Infused with creativity, surprise elements, and stunning crafts-manship, their collections blend intentional design with quality materials, instilling future heirlooms with enduring and useful life cycles. *arteriorshome.com*

BRABBU
An avant-garde brand with a diverse range of well-crafted furniture, casegoods, upholstery, lighting, and rugs. *brabbu.com*

COCO REPUBLIC
This Australian brand encapsulates effortless luxury, crafting furniture inspired by the global community while maintaining its commitment to quality. *cocorepublic.com*

CUFF STUDIO
The Los Angeles–based furniture and lighting design studio is known for its inviting angles, curves, and architectural elements. *cuffstudio.com*

EGG COLLECTIVE
A New York–based design house creating heirloom-quality, locally made pieces with a focus on sculptural forms and natural materials. *eggcollective.com*

EICHHOLTZ
Clean lines, modern silhouettes, and fresh material combinations blend subtly with contemporary interpre-tations of classic typologies at this Dutch furniture and lighting brand. *eichholtz.com*

FYRN*
The heritage studio combines traditional woodworking principles with modern techniques, including patented joinery, and focuses a great deal on waste and durability for future generations. *fyrn.com*

IAN ALISTAIR COCHRAN

The artist's happy-hued, bubble-like resin furniture first debuted at Fernando Mastrangelo Studio's exhibition, "In Good Company," emphasizing material awareness and shapely experimentation. *iancochran.com*

INDUSTRY WEST

The Southern brand reinterprets modern furniture trends at a price point that makes its creations accessible to more people. *industrywest.com*

THE INVISIBLE COLLECTION

An always exciting collection of iconic furniture pieces from the biggest names in design, past and present. *theinvisiblecollection.com*

JONATHAN ADLER

This design star is known for his whimsical pottery, but I have always loved his glamorous spin on mid-century furniture. *jonathanadler.com*

KELLY WEARSTLER

The multidisciplinary team thrives on creative cross-pollination, shaping meticulously detailed architecture, interiors, and a diverse range of products from furniture to textiles. *kellywearstler.com*

LOVE HOUSE

Founded by visual arts enthusiasts Jared Heinrich and Aric Yeakey, the showroom celebrates contemporary designers of custom and limited-edition pieces. *lovehouseny.com*

LUCY KURREIN

Marrying industrial precision with historical design references to achieve her signature slender silhouettes, this artist focuses on material tactility from her studio in Paris. *lucykurrein.com*

MARBERA

Headquartered in Paris, crafted in Italy. Marbera transforms the world's finest stones (marble, onyx) into colorful, sculptural furniture. *marbera-studio.com*

MONTANA FURNITURE*

These talented artisans in Denmark are known for their modular systems, which are certified with the EU Ecolabel, and use water-based lacquer colors free of harmful solvents. *montanafurniture.com*

MOROSO

Producers of some of the most historically recognizable furniture of our time. Its continued collaborations with industry leaders (Patricia Urquiola, Ron Arad) make it an international force. *moroso.it*

MOUS

Founded by siblings Tanner Moussa and Mackenzie Lewis, the studio is powered by generations of design heritage and blends old-world techniques with new-world aesthetics. *mousstudio.com*

NELLA VETRINA**

A showroom dedicated to everything there is to love about luxury Italian furniture. *nellavetrina.com*

ROVE CONCEPTS*

The Pacific Northwest brand goes beyond furniture design by connecting luxury and sustainability, driving meaningful change with its eco-friendly practices and natural materials. *roveconcepts.com*

SEDGWICK & BRATTLE**

Thom Filicia's to-the-trade showroom offers new and vintage upholstery, lighting, artwork, bedding, and more, cultivating inspired environments for authentic living. *sedgwickandbrattle.com*

SUN AT SIX*

Using FSC-certified woods, rapidly renewable bamboo, and Oeko-Tex Standard 100 fabrics, the artisans at this sustainable furniture studio are masters in the rich tradition of Chinese joinery. *sunatsix.com*

THOMAS HAYES STUDIO

A handmade collection of modern furniture that takes cues from the California Craftsman revolution and mid-century Brazilian design. *thomashayesstudio.com*

WOVEN*

Embracing "home" as an ever-evolving journey, this collection of nature-inspired furniture, lighting, and accessories is crafted with mindful materials meant to last for generations. *wovenshop.com*

HARDWARE

BUSTER + PUNCH

What began as a love for crafting motorbikes has turned into an obsession with elevating home fittings, like textured brass dimmers and toggle switches. *busterandpunch.com*

CALIFORNIA FAUCETS*

The recyclable solid brass faucets produced by this family-owned company are created with clean air, waste management, water conservation, and LEED requirements top of mind. *calfaucets.com*

BALDWIN HARDWARE*

A member of the U.S. EPA's National Partnership for Environmental Priorities, this brand responsibly crafts brass hardware in more than twenty finishes. *baldwinhardware.com*

DUTTON BROWN

Made to order in Minneapolis, this brand's hardware selection reinvents classic designs and empowers customers to personalize their spaces with vibrant color choices. *duttonbrown.com*

EMTEK

From terrazzo levers to 3D-printed metal patterns inspired by nature, this Los Angeles–based hardware studio finds inspiration in the everyday. *emtek.com*

MATILDA GOAD & CO.

With a design approach that reinvents tradition, this British atelier drums up charming embellishments in knobs, pulls, and backplates for a fresh look. *matildagoad.com*

MORGIK METAL DESIGNS**

Specializing in wrought iron, brass, and stainless steel, this custom manufacturer crafts decorative drapery hardware and architectural metalwork for interior and exterior spaces. *morgik.com*

PLANK HARDWARE*

As a Certified B Corp, this carbon neutral studio minimizes or offsets its carbon footprint while producing classic and artistic hardware solutions. *us.plankhardware.com*

SCHAUB & COMPANY

The use of precious inlays and ornate carvings is what sets the cabinet hardware from this Midwestern brand apart. *schaubandcompany.com*

Macaroni drawer pulls by Sam Stewart.

Moirai Chandelier by Ini Archibong.

GABRIEL SCOTT
This artisan studio in Montreal creates modular, made-to-order configurations that are highly customizable and collaborative. *gabriel-scott.com*

IN COMMON WITH
Working with global artisans and engineers, Nick Ozemba and Felicia Hung design bespoke light fixtures that can be configured in a multitude of ways. *incommonwith.com*

JOHN POMP**
Molten glass, warped metal, and refracted light marry to create organic forms that appear almost otherworldly when lit. *johnpomp.com*

LINDSEY ADELMAN
Combining organic, handwrought materials, like blown glass, with the strong industrial beauty of machine-milled components, her lighting systems create warmth and drama. *lindseyadelman.com*

MERVE KAHRAMAN
Handcrafted in Istanbul, each design has a story to tell, from space exploration to a wax lamp that continually reinvents itself. *mervekahraman.com*

PELLE
A Brooklyn design studio that combines the practices of art and engineering to create expressive and sculptural light fixtures. *pelledesigns.com*

RBW LIGHTING*/**
Crafting lighting experiences that go beyond illumination, each creation from this Certified B Corp supports the belief that light affects our mental and physical well-being. *rbw.com*

SKLO*
These light fixtures are rooted in centuries-old Czech tradition yet exhibit a California-minded modern twist. *sklo.com*

VISUAL COMFORT & CO.
A range of traditional and contemporary fixtures created by renowned designers and led by "lighting legend" Earle F. Chapman. *visualcomfort.com*

SUN VALLEY BRONZE*
Each piece of hardware is crafted from art-grade bronze, using at least 85 percent pre-consumer recycled material, resulting in designs that truly endure. *sunvalleybronze.com*

THG PARIS*
Gemstone inlays, gold-stamped crystal, and white porcelain mark a commitment to luxury, while sustainable production processes around recycling and renewable energy show care for the planet. *thg-paris.com*

WATERMARK DESIGNS*
State-of-the-art technology meets hands-on craft at this Brooklyn-based studio, which is known for its water-saving features and collaborations with architects and designers. *watermark-designs.com*

WATERWORKS
High-end, meticulously designed kitchen and bath fittings (in dozens of finishes) are what this industry leader is known for. *waterworks.com*

LIGHTING

ANDLIGHT
The Copenhagen-based online retailer specializes in designer lighting from artisanal brands and considers light a central source of hygge, the Danish concept of joy. *andlight.com*

APPARATUS
Aged brass, marble, horsehair, and porcelain are combined to create modern light fixtures that fuse sculptural shapes with hand-worn materials. *apparatusstudio.com*

ARETI
Drawing on their backgrounds in visual arts, architecture, and design, two sisters joined forces to create pieces that explore curiosity and emotion. *atelierareti.com*

ATELIER DE TROUPE
Hand-finished in Los Angeles, each fixture draws inspiration from Modernism, Art Deco, and cinema with a focus on natural materials. *atelierdetroupe.com*

CHRISTINA Z ANTONIO
Known for pushing material boundaries, this New York City studio creates the sort of statement lighting that always pops. *christinazantonio.com*

CIRCA
The team here brings a meticulous eye to its approach to design, creating sculptural pendants and multi-tiered chandeliers with an incredible attention to detail. *circainteriors.com*

CURRENT*
Pioneers in LED technology and smart controls, the brand's sustainability efforts extend beyond energy consumption with inclusive and ethical corporate policies. *currentlighting.com*

EMPTYOO
Offering iconic and contemporary cordless lamps with LED lighting, these luminaires are meant to be as energy-efficient and long-lasting as they are stylish. *emptyoo.com*

ENY LEE PARKER
Everything this ceramicist and designer touches turns to gold, including her sculptural lighting. *enyleeparker.com*

FOUNDRY
Whether your aesthetic leans more mid-century or contemporary, this resource for European and American lighting designs has been curated to complement any interior. *foundrylighting.com*

Modern Love paint splotch by Backdrop.

A wild arrangement of my favorite pinks by Eric Buterbaugh in Los Angeles.

PAINT

ANNIE SLOAN
The color expert is known for her Chalk Paint collection in an array of beautiful hues. *anniesloan.com*

BACKDROP*
The Climate Neutral Certified brand boasts low-VOC and Green Wise–certified paints for interiors, exteriors, and cabinets, and invests in social impact initiatives. *backdrophome.com*

BENJAMIN MOORE
Pioneering and proprietary color technologies make this brand an MVP in the paint game, driving color trends and continuing to innovate since 1883. *benjaminmoore.com*

CLARE*
This woman- and minority-owned business makes color-curated, water-based paints with zero VOCs and prioritizes well-being and indoor air quality. *clare.com*

COAT*
High-grade ingredients ensure a velvety smooth finish for this Certified B Corp and Climate Positive brand. Even the regenerative bamboo paint brushes are sustainable. *coatpaints.com*

FARROW & BALL*
Known for its rich pigments and eco-conscious approach, this British heritage brand embraces artisanal methods and water-based finishes. *farrow-ball.com*

FINE PAINTS OF EUROPE
This family-owned paint purveyor delivers top-quality, pigmented Dutch paints from the Netherlands. *finepaintsofeurope.com*

KILZ
In collaboration with Magnolia Home and Joanna Gaines, Kilz debuted a premium paint line that embodies the designer's timeless and relaxed style. *kilz.com*

LICK*
With sustainability and community at its core, the Climate Neutral, Certified B Corp produces water-based, low-VOC paints and gives back by supporting water charities. *lick.com*

PANTONE
Providing a universal visual language to designers and paint producers, the preeminent color resource promotes consistency through formula guides and color stories. *pantone.com*

PORTOLA PAINTS*
In the heart of Los Angeles, this eco-friendly brand creates saturated palettes and specialty finishes with no VOCs in small batches blended by hand. *portolapaints.com*

PLANTS + FLOWERS

BLOOMIST*
A passion for nature, social impact, and eco-conscious design drives this purveyor of ethically sourced artisanal goods and plants that transform homes into sanctuaries of well-being. *bloomist.com*

BRECK'S
A mail-order gardening company that imports Dutch bulbs cultivated in the fields of Holland, including alliums, tulips, and amaryllis. *brecks.com*

BOUQS*
Responsibly sourced, farm-fresh florals paired with a generous dose of kindness toward others and the planet. *bouqs.com*

CANOPY PLANT CO.
Lovingly cared for in New Orleans by founders Ben Callender and Ryan Nash, these high-quality, pest-free tropical plants nourish the mind and spirit. *canopyplantco.com*

DAHING PLANTS
This New York–based greenery shop provides convenient next-day delivery services, allowing customers to make informed choices via live photos and accurate plant dimension listings. *dahingplants.com*

ERIC BUTERBAUGH
It's hard to say who is bringing the bigger personality punch at this LA flower institution, the explosive arrangements or the charismatic owner. Either way, I'm obsessed with the creative florals coming out of this shop. *ericbuterbaugh.com*

FLOOM
The innovative online flower delivery platform celebrates the artistry of arrangements by partnering with talented local florists. *floom.com*

JOMO STUDIO
I'm obsessed with this Toronto-based plant delivery service. It not only has an impressive assortment but also offers some of the most helpful tips on caring for your leafy green friends. (Sadly, it currently only delivers in Canada.) *jomostudio.com*

LEAF & CLAY*
If their massive selection of succulents wasn't enough, they also factor in their impact on the environment by recycling nursery pots and reducing CO_2 emissions. *leafandclay.co*

LÉON & GEORGE
Dedicated to reuniting city dwellers with nature, the plant service provides hand-selected, California-grown greenery sourced from trusted local growers. *leonandgeorge.com*

LET'S GET TO IT

RUGS

ARMADILLO*
This Australian brand is a purpose-led Certified B Corp loved for its handmade rugs and dedication to ancient craftsmanship. armadillo-co.com

KNOTS RUGS*
The third-generation fair trade rug company based in London creates statement floor coverings hand-knotted in Nepal using Tibetan wool and Chinese silk. knotsrugs.co.uk

L&M CUSTOM CARPETS
From flat weaves to kilims to hand-tufted wool, this company redefines carpets, focusing on quality and service through bespoke designs and custom sizing. lmcustomcarpets.com

NORDIC KNOTS
Designed in Stockholm and handcrafted in India, the Goodweave-certified textile brand offers a collection of modern rugs rooted in timeless Scandinavian principles. nordicknots.com

PATTERSON FLYNN**
Driven by craftsmanship and exquisite artistry, this is the place to find interesting textural explorations and traditional patterns in modern color combinations. pattersonflynn.com

PERENNIALS**
These mold-resistant performance rugs blend luxury and functionality, providing easy care and durability while being customizable to fit any space. perennialsfabrics.com

ROSEMARY HALLGARTEN
Famous for her alpaca rugs, the designer has always revered texture and craft, and continues to support artisans in Peru, Brazil, and Nepal. rosemaryhallgarten.com

RUG ART
This curated collection of contemporary rugs blends bold patterns and minimalist styles. Each rug is hand-knotted in Nepal by local artisans. rugart.nyc

RUG COUTURE
Each customizable rug tells a distinct story through carefully selected materials, expert weaving, and collaborative efforts between clients, designers, and craftspeople. rugcouture.com

STARK
This luxury rug dynasty once outfitted the White House and today creates collections with some of the industry's top interior designers. starkcarpet.com

THE RUG COMPANY
It takes a minimum of four months to make one of its fine, hand-knotted rugs, each woven with wool from a Tibetan plateau using traditional techniques. therugcompany.com

WOVEN
A curation of storied antiques and sublime tribal designs, this studio creates handwoven rugs that live harmoniously alongside its global discoveries. woven.is

An Opera D'Arte marble sample from ABC Stone.

Custom rug design by The Rug Company.

STONE

ABC STONE*
This New York–based showroom is reshaping the stone landscape with their diverse material portfolio. Don't miss the Classic Rock Collection, an assortment of furniture and bathroom fixtures – designed by moi. abcworldwidestone.com

ANN SACKS
Known for their design-forward collaborations, the brand fosters creativity, exploration, and the pursuit of great design. annsacks.com

ARCA STUDIO
A creative international stone hub with operations in Miami. They are most loved for their envelope-pushing collaborations with leaders in the design, culture, and art worlds. arcaww.com

BAS STONE
A women-owned supplier that prizes character over all else, this is the place to find rare, globally sourced stone hand-picked by its founders. basstonenyc.com

MARBLE UNLIMITED
The largest stone supplier on the West Coast, they source exotic stones from more than twenty-five countries including Italy, Portugal, Turkey, and Brazil. marbleunlimitedinc.com

NEW YORK STONE
More than five hundred types of stone on hand – and twenty thousand slabs in stock. This is where quality meets design expertise meets global shipping capabilities. newyorkstone.com

PMI INTERNATIONAL STONE IMPORTERS
A go-to destination for natural stone slabs and engineered quartz on the East Coast. pmirock.com

ROYAL STONE & TILE*
This family-owned slab yard in Los Angeles has a classic range of quality stones and specializes in Italian materials such as Carrera and Calacatta marbles. royalstonela.com

STONELAND USA
A Hollywood, California, supplier that handpicks each stone based on its quality, aesthetic appeal, and specific customer design needs. stonelandusa.com

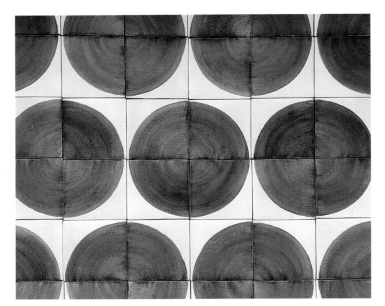

Hand-painted Crest Tiles by Riad Tile.

TILE

ARTISTIC TILE
Turning tile installation into an art form, this luxury brand produces thousands of customizable materials and designs. I especially love their innovative partnerships with industry creatives. *artistictile.com*

CLÉ TILE*
Heirloom-quality tiles by the leader in artisanal offerings, from Moroccan to penny rounds to styles with special, hand-chiseled finishes. *cletile.com*

DALTILE*
A leading US manufacturer with an expansive library — from the highly functional to the design forward — all created with a promise to make beautiful tile responsibly. *daltile.com*

DW TILE & STONE**
The exclusive collections feature intricate patterns like Calacatta Gold marble or brass mosaics with travertine. *dwtileandstone.com*

FIRECLAY TILE*
A Northern California–based brand that is reshaping the industry by integrating sustainable practices and recycled materials into their production. *fireclaytile.com*

MONTECERA
A global leader in the stone industry with a diverse selection of premium porcelain, natural stone, and captivating mosaic tiles. *montecera.com*

NASCO
They have a quick-ship program that ensures their expansive selection of in-stock colors, finishes, and styles arrive in record time. Don't miss their Love Bars collection. *nascostonetile.com*

PLASTICIET*
Transforming recycled plastics into stunning surface panels, this sustainable pioneer out of Rotterdam draws inspiration from natural stone while striving to co-create a post-waste world. *plasticiet.com*

RIAD TILE
From cold-cured cement to hand-polished marble to high-quality terrazzo, the Dallas-based studio offers a well-rounded variety of surfaces. *riadtile.com*

TILEBAR
They are known for their wide array of materials, from porcelain, ceramic, glass, and terrazzo to natural stone, all sourced globally. *tilebar.com*

USA TILE & MARBLE
With an extensive product range including slate, granite, mosaics, wood, laminate, ceramic, marble, and porcelain tiles, the family-owned staple is one of Miami's top tile destinations. *usatileandmarble.net*

WALLPAPER

ABA INTERIORS*
With a selection of metallic foils, grasscloths, and textured paper weaves, this family-owned studio creates a tactile experience rooted in innovation. *abainteriors.com*

ABIGAIL EDWARDS*
Hand-drawn patterns that nod to nature's beauty and the whimsy of fairy tales come alive in these UK-crafted, sustainably minded wallpapers created with nontoxic, water-based inks. *abigailedwards.com*

ABNORMALS ANONYMOUS
Life's ordinary moments become extraordinary as coastal cues and playful flora-and-fauna motifs transform the everyday into magical wonders filled with curiosity. *abnormalsanonymous.com*

AREA ENVIRONMENTS
Dreamlike watercolors. Sculptural canvasses. Nature-inspired musings. This studio collaborates with artists to turn their original works into wallpapers and large-scale murals. *areaenvironments.com*

ASHLEY WOODSON BAILEY
Poppies, peonies, and camellias bloom in oversized arrangements to form dramatic, moody backdrops with a photographic appeal and a touch of romance. *awblove.com*

ASTEK HOME*
A zero-VOC printing process, color-matching capabilities, and hi-tech effects that mimic textures (think embossing and brushstrokes) ensure an eco-friendly and artistic result. *astekhome.com*

ASTERÉ
Merging Surrealism, abstraction, objets d'art, and architectural elements into mural-like wallcoverings that look like they belong in a gallery. *astere.fr*

ATELIER RSH
A nod to the Parisian art of blending the very old with the very new, these wallcoverings celebrate color, texture, and pattern through graphic designs rendered in dusty palettes. *atelierrsh.com*

CALICO WALLPAPER
Immersive environmental murals that explore everything from ethereal ombrés to NASA's celestial satellite imagery. *calicowallpaper.com*

CAVERN HOME
From Sunset Boulevard Toile de Jouys to bunnies and bows, these hand-screened prints bring a sweet stamp to interiors using eco-friendly, water-based inks. *cavernhome.com*

CASADECO
This French collection of wallpapers and panoramics pulls color and design inspiration from Mother Nature, varying time periods, and exotic destinations. *casadeco.com*

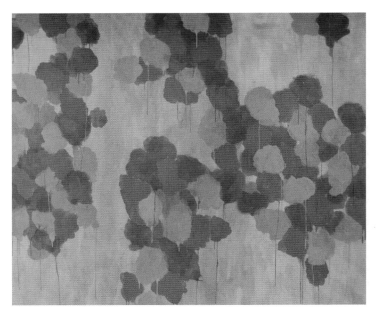

Floral Graffiti hand-painted wallpaper by Porter Teleo.

CHASING PAPER*
High-quality removable options redefine peel-and-stick wallpaper while permanent solutions cater to the traditional fold; all are low VOC, phthalate-free, and printed using Greenguard gold-certified inks. *chasingpaper.com*

CHEZ SHEA
Folding and dyeing paper by hand—the art of orizome—allows for intentional-yet-spontaneous expression, ensuring no pattern is exactly the same. *chezsheadesign.com*

COPE*
Experimentation reigns supreme as nature, art, and science converge using traditional techniques, modern sensibilities, and sustainable elements (think clay-coated, FSC-certified paper). *studiocope.com*

COWTAN & TOUT**
Timeless elegance gets a modern twist with an American point of view in this eclectic collection of woven and vinyl wallcoverings. *cowtan.com*

DESIGNERS GUILD**
The artistically inclined atelier delivers diverse collections featuring exquisite florals, chic geometrics, and flocked damasks. *designersguild.com*

DESIGNTEX*
These papers are digitally printed in Maine, where a team of artists, technologists, and craftspeople collaborate with social responsibility top of mind. *designtex.com*

DROP IT MODERN
Fresh color palettes and artisanal prints draw on memories, architecture, and travels at this woman-owned business that seeks to elicit joy and ignite creativity. *dropitmodern.com*

ÉLITIS
Available through Urban Wallcovering, Élitis presents elegant and contemporary selections in a variety of finishes including grasscloth, glass beads, 3D panels, and wood veneers. *urbanwallcovering.com*

ELIZABETH DOW
The tonal quality of these papers speaks to the sophisticated use of texture, color, and light for which their namesake designer is known. *elizabethdow.com*

ERICA WAKERLY
This British designer's creations add glints of reflective, metallic sheen to interiors and are inspired by a minimalist ethos and architectural sensibilities. *ericawakerlywallpaper.com*

ESO STUDIO*
Fabrics that are naturally dyed using plants, minerals, and organic materials are translated into digitally printed wallpaper patterns. *esostudioshop.com*

EVER ATELIER
Ashley Leftwich and Sarah English have transformed their shared passion for color, pattern, and art into designs that evoke emotional responses. *everatelier.com*

FLAT VERNACULAR*
Pattern makes perfect at this design studio known for its playful aesthetic and ability to translate original art onto FSC-certified paper using low-VOC inks. *flatvernacular.com*

FLAVOR PAPER*
Innovative materials and technologies (think holograms and scratch-and-sniff scents) defy convention on these conversational wallpapers that are made-to-order and use eco-friendly, water-based inks. *flavorpaper.com*

FRENCH AMERICAN WALLPAPER
Original artwork-turned-bespoke murals, these luxury papers are custom-printed in Los Angeles and feature color stories influenced by all things French. *frenchamericanwallpaper.com*

FROMENTAL**
Hand-painting and hand-embroidery transform raw silk canvases into exquisite panels, while their printed offerings conjure the same painterly quality. *fromental.co.uk*

GRACIE
With a legacy dating back to 1898, this ultra-bespoke studio paints each scenic design by hand, honoring a three-hundred-year-old craft. *graciestudio.com*

GROW HOUSE GROW*
Each hand silk-screened pattern tells a visual fairy tale with a happy ending that sees one tree planted for every roll of wallpaper sold (thanks to an initiative called One Tree Planted). *growhousegrow.com*

HEATHER JOZAK STUDIOS
Bespoke finishes from lime plasters and washes to hand-applied metal leafing turn surfaces into decorative works of art. *heatherjozakstudios.com*

HOVIA*
Nontoxic inks and toners support the environmentally friendly foundations of these ethically sourced wallpapers, digitally printed in Liverpool. *hovia.com*

ISIDORE LEROY
Pioneering technological advances even in 1842, this French textile house continues to innovate, producing artistic designs via traditional roller printing and digital techniques. *isidoreleroy.com*

JILL MALEK**
Dimensional materials and nature-inspired patterns promote wellness, restoration, and tranquility, turning interior environments into human-centric havens. *jillmalek.com*

JILL SEALE DESIGN STUDIO
Artisanal wallpapers reflect a fashion-forward point of view. I'm especially drawn to her colorful, oversized marbled patterns. *jillseale.com*

KERRI ROSENTHAL
Bold and playful artworks that feel like pure joy are reimagined into wallcoverings marked by authenticity, individuality, and an unending love of color. *kerrirosenthal.com*

KIRKBY DESIGN*/**
Mindful materials like FSC-certified wood pulp, renewable corn fiber, cork, and hemp give bold graphics and pigmented palettes a hit of big, touchable texture. *kirkbydesign.com*

KNOLL TEXTILES*
High-performance woven, vinyl, and specialty wallcoverings support the brand's corporate sustainability efforts, which address environmental, economic, and social impact. *knoll.com*

KRISTY STAFFORD
Informed by her background in art and fashion, this designer channels her passion for pattern and color into harmonious compositions that radiate energy. *kristystafford.com*

LOUEE VEGA
This Charleston-based design studio features hand-painted and hand-dyed patterns by founder Caroline Bradley, all with a coastal vibe. *loueevega.com*

MAKELIKE
Based in Portland, Oregon, this multidisciplinary graphic design studio crafts illustrative and covetable wallpapers that pack a sophisticated punch. *makelike.com*

MAYA ROMANOFF*/**
Expect the unexpected from these philanthropic-minded creators. Glass beads, seashells, even pigmented woods are used to create innovative—and sustainable—wallcoverings. *mayaromanoff.com*

MEGAN ADAMS BROOKS**
I love her impressive exploration of materiality, in vegan leather, paper weaves, linen, metallic, and grasscloth wallpapers. *meganadamsbrooks.com*

MITCHELL BLACK
Founded by Lynai Jones, the studio evolved from a stationery company into a dynamic surface brand offering graphic wallpapers and painterly murals. *mitchellblack.com*

MJ ATELIER**
Artist Maria Apelo Cruz works with husband Mike Jovanovic to create custom bas-relief plaster wallcoverings sculpted by hand. *mjatelier.com*

NAMA ROCOCO
Colorfully bold, contemporary designs produced with museum-quality materials and sold in single sheets. *namarococo.com*

NEWWALL
Scouring the globe for distinctive designs, Maria Raco and team curate fashionable, on-trend wallcoverings. *newwall.com*

NINA CAMPBELL**
The iconic designer elevates spaces with her exquisite fabric and wallcoverings. Embodying a blend of luxury, practicality, and wit, her sought-after collections feel timeless and bold. *ninacampbell.com*

NOBILIS**
A signature element of French interior design since 1928, these collections are characterized by elegant geometrics, expressive botanicals, and an element of curiosity. *nobilis.fr*

OLIVIA + POPPY
Graphic lines, bold patterns, and clever, cheeky motifs done in sophisticated hues that brighten walls and spark conversation. *oliviaandpoppy.com*

OONSAI*
Combining Korean heritage with West Coast vibes, these hand-painted wallcoverings are responsibly created using FSC-certified paper, biodegradable sisal grasscloth, and water-based inks. *oonsai.com*

OSBORNE & LITTLE**
This design studio employs innovative techniques to create collections that read classic and contemporary, featuring everything from geometrics to florals, damasks to stripes. *osborneandlittle.com*

PAPER MILLS*/**
Founded by Amy Mills, this art and design house manufactures custom wallpapers by hand, using recycled content and no-VOC paints. *papermills.net*

THE PATTERN COLLECTIVE
This woman-owned textile studio out of New Orleans has a thing for wild patterns and hand-painted watercolor designs. *thepatterncollective.com*

PHILOMELA
Original textiles balance the delicate with the daring through intricate hand-drawn, painted, and printed patterns. *philomelasweb.com*

POPPY
Jennifer Hunt employs a vibrant fusion of art in her animated and unexpected wallpaper designs that bring life and energy to spaces. *poppyprintstudio.com*

PORTER TELEO**
Distinctive hand-painted and hand-printed wallcoverings and fabrics inspired by a variety of art processes and traditions. *porterteleo.com*

QUERCUS & CO.*
Hand-painted imperfection meets the precision of modern technology in this collection that uses ethically sourced materials and responsible manufacturing processes. *quercusandco.com*

ROBERT CROWDER
An industry powerhouse, the brand blends style, quality, and a unique design sensibility when creating their high-end, bespoke wall treatments. *robertcrowder.com*

SCHUMACHER**
Innovating for more than 130 years, this textile house honors the past while embracing the future in a commitment to designs that transcend time. *schumacher.com*

SIAN ZENG
Enchanting, dreamlike illustrations that recall the artist's childhood love for children's folktales. *sianzeng.com*

STUDIO E*/**
With Venetian plaster and metallic offerings, this specialty line is crafted by hand, using elements from nature, recycled materials, and water-borne paints. *studioeinc.com*

STUDIO MOSES
The artistic prowess of this multi-disciplinary surface studio is clear in its thoughtful patterns that nod to the worlds of architecture, interiors, and fashion. *studiomosesny.com*

STUDIO PRINTWORKS
With a mantra like "boldly wallpaper" to live up to, this studio taps master screen printers and colorists to handcraft high-style designs that invigorate the soul. *studioprintworks.com*

SURFACES BY DAVID BONK**
Custom, multi-layered artisan wallpapers that include intricate details such as hand-applied metallic or pearl finishes. *surfacesbydavidbonk.com*

TANIA VARTAN
Drawing inspiration from her 1970s dress fabrics, this seasoned fashion designer-turned-muralist brings her background in textiles and decorative arts to life. *taniavartan.com*

THATCHER*
As a certified Climate Neutral brand, Avery Thatcher's design studio treads lightly on the planet, crafting outré wallcoverings that prove opposites attract. *thatcherstudio.com*

THESE WALLS*
Made in Australia with recycled and renewable materials, these storied wallpapers capture the essence of lovingly lived-in spaces and the memories created within. *thesewalls.com.au*

TOMMA BLOOM
Textile design becomes a visual language as form and color are reimagined into wallcoverings, upholstery fabrics, rugs, and tiles. *tommabloom.com*

VAHALLAN**
Fearless experimentation leads skilled artisans to meticulously hand-craft luxury wallpapers with innovation, creativity, and passion. *vahallan.com*

VICTORIA LARSON
A visual storyteller, this artist fashions wallpapers that speak to her love of art and the magic of the sea. *victoria-larson.com*

VOUTSA*/**
This collection is continually evolving at the intersection of art history and modern manufacturing with an eye toward environmental and social impact. *voutsa.com*

WALLPAPER PROJECTS
The experimental studio explores unique materials and techniques, collaborating with brands, artists, and individuals to create custom wallpapers that double as immersive art installations. *wallpaperprojects.com*

WINDOW TREATMENTS

THE FAIR CUSTOM WINDOW FASHIONS
The Queens-based company believes that creating custom window treatments should be easy, which is why it works closely with clients from vision to installation. *thefaircustom.com*

HORIZONS
A trusted design-industry favorite because of its unerring attention to detail and impressive ability to dress even the trickiest window configurations. *horizonshades.com*

HUNTER DOUGLAS
The latest in window treatment technologies, from hidden energy-efficient layers to motorized controls, in a stylish selection of shades, shutters, and blinds. *hunterdouglas.com*

THE SHADE STORE
In addition to handcrafting custom window treatments, the brand makes an impact with organizations like the Arbor Day Foundation, which plants a tree for every order placed. *theshadestore.com*

Custom window treatments featuring Kelly Wearstler's Graffito fabric.

PHOTOGRAPHY CREDITS

A thousand thank-yous to all the incredibly talented designers, makers, and photographers, whose work is featured in this book.

Page 1 Photo by Matthieu Salvaing; design by Corinne Sachot and Gabriel Kowalski.

Pages 2, 77 Design by Bettencourt Manor.

Pages 4–5 Photo by Matthieu Salvaing, design by Mathieu Lehanneur.

Page 6 Design by Undercurrent Studio.

Pages 8–9, 21, 27, 116–117 Photos by Brian Wetzel; design by Cara Woodhouse.

Page 10 Photo by Dean Hearne; design by Henry Holland.

Pages 12–13 Photo by Clemens Poloczek; design by Sabine Marcelis.

Page 14 Photo by Stephan Julliard; design by Le Berre Vevaud.

Page 17 Photo by Ian Vecchiotti; chairs courtesy of South Loop Loft.

Pages 18–19 Photo by Felipe Ribon; design by Mathieu Lehanneur.

Pages 22, 23, 88, 89, 121, 122, 123, 144–145, 175, 176, 177, 198–199 Photos by Genevieve Garruppo; design by Cara Woodhouse.

Page 26 Design by Merve Kahraman.

Page 28 Photo by Jake Curtis, *House & Garden* © Condé Nast; design by Gabby Deeming and Ruth Sleightholme.

Page 29 Top: photo by Diana Paulson. Bottom: photo by Vera Nilsson/ferm LIVING.

Page 30 Design by Guilherme Torre.

Page 31 Photo by Claire Esparros; design by Marc Houston.

Pages 32–33 Photo by Patrick Locqueneux/ Mr. Tripper; property via iconic.house

Page 34 Design by Studio Frey AG.

Page 35 Photo by Bruce Damonte.

Page 37 Photo by Madeline Tolle for StudioProba; pool mural by Alex Proba of StudioProba Inc.

Page 38 Photo by Jon Bilous/Alamy.

Page 39 Photo by Casey Dunn Photography/ Sit and Look Studios Inc.; architecture by alterstudio.

Pages 40, 210–211 Photos by Pernille Loof/Trunk Archive; design by Rafael de Cárdenas for Ulla Johnson.

Page 41 Photo by Nicole Franzen.

Pages 43, 64–65, 92, 164, 170–171, 184, 208, 218, 224–225, 270, 282 Design by Cara Woodhouse.

Pages 45, 67, 95, 119, 147, 173, 201, 227 Photos by Joanna McClure; styling by Cara Gibbs and Cara Woodhouse.

Pages 47, 48, 49 Photos by Lauren Bamford; design collaboration with Hearth Studio.

Page 53 Photo courtesy of Studio Kai Linke; tile production by Kaufmann Keramik GmbH.

Page 54 Photo by Anson Smart; design by Alexander &CO.

Page 55 Photo by David Raffoul; interior design by david/nicolas for KZB Residence in Amman, Jordan.

Page 57 Photo by Anson Smart; design by Greg Natale.

Page 58 Photo by Chris Mottalini; design by Charlap Hyman & Herrero.

Page 59 Photo by Michael Sinclair, *House & Garden* © Condé Nast; design by Pandora Taylor.

Page 60 Photo by Jeff Holt; design by Fawn Galli.

Page 61 Photo by Chris Mottalini; design by Oliver Freundlich.

Page 62 Photo by Black & Steil; Rock Light 06, 2023, by Lindsey Adelman.

Page 63 Photo by Michael Clifford; hand-painted "Namban" wallpaper in polished copper colorway by de Gournay.

Pages 69, 71 Photos by Melanie Acevedo.

Page 70 Photo by Marion Brenner; design by Andrea Cochran Landscape Architecture.

Page 74 Photo by Anson Smart; design by SJB.

Page 76 Design by Janaína Araújo Arquitetura e Interiores.

Pages 78–79 Photo by Chris Mottalini.

Page 81 Top left: design by Kelly Wearstler; top right: photo by Karel Balas; bottom: photo of Wiggle Bench courtesy of Studio Sam Klemick.

Page 83 Photo by Anson Smart for Armadillo.

Page 84 Photo by Julien Fernandez/Gap Interiors.

Page 85 Vase series by Karen Gayle Tinney.

Page 86 Photo by Joshua McHugh; design by Elena Frampton of Frampton Co.

Page 87 Photo by Greg Cox for Bureaux; design by Atelier du Pont; textile and ceramic mural by artisans Jaume Roig and Adriana Meunié.

Page 90 Photo by Daniel Schäfer Photography.

Page 91 Photo courtesy of Ryan Belli and Tim Hans.

"Curly" lamp by Gustaf Westman. Bottom row, right: Photo courtesy of Friedman Benda and Fernando Laposse; "Pink Furry Armchair," 2022, by Fernando Laposse.

Page 233 Photo by Denis Lesak/Unsplash.

Page 237 Photo of Soda SQ courtesy of Miniforms; design by Yiannis Ghikas.

Page 238 Photo by Stephen Kent Johnson/ OTTO; design by Kelly Behun.

Page 241 Top row, left: photo by Matthew Donaldson; "Fudge" chair by Faye Toogood. Top row, center: image by digital artist Ezequiel Pini of Six N. Five. Top row, right: photo of "Stacked" sculptures courtesy of Annie Morris. Middle row, left: photo of "Totem" lights courtesy of Sabine Marcelis. Middle row, center: photo of "Balance" courtesy of Vanessa Barragão. Middle row, right: photo of Haas Brothers "Butts Up" box courtesy of L'Objet. Bottom row, left: photo by Brian Wetzel; interior design by WIDELL + BOSCHETTI; "Arc" dining chairs by Cuff Studio. Bottom row, center: photo of sculpture courtesy of Jess Murphy. Bottom row, right: coupes image courtesy of the ClubRoom/Invisible Collection.

Pages 242–243, 252–253 Photos by Gabriel Zimmer; styling by Kate Bergeron. Crystals courtesy of Bodhi Holistic Spa in Hudson, New York.

Pages 244–245, 256–257 Photos by Gabriel Zimmer; styling by Kate Bergeron.

Pages 246, 247, 248–249, 250, 251 All photos by Julieanne Browning/Pine & Fable; styling by Kate Bergeron.

Pages 254, 255 All photos by Julieanne Browning/Pine & Fable; styling by Kate Bergeron. Crystals courtesy of Bodhi Holistic Spa in Hudson, New York.

Page 258 Left: *Crassula pellucida* photo by A_Gree/Alamy. Center: *Cleistocactus coladomononis* photo by areeya_ann/Shutterstock. Right: *Cotyledon pendens* photo by Emily LaPatra/Magic Valley Gardens.

Page 259 Left: *Crassula marnieriana* photo by Kay Roxby/Alamy. Center: *Sedum morganianum* photo by Dorling Kindersley ltd/Alamy. Right: *Curio rowleyanus* photo by olga Yastremska/ Alamy.

Page 260 Left: basil photo by Lasse Kristensen/ Alamy. Center: mint photo by Maksim Lashcheuski/Alamy. Right: rosemary photo by Oleksii Terpugov/Alamy.

Page 261 Left: sage photo by Panther Media GmbH/Alamy. Center: Thai basil photo by Arthit Buarapa/Alamy. Right: thyme photo by Lasse Kristensen/Alamy.

Page 262 Left: bird of paradise photo courtesy of JOMO Studio; jomostudio.com. Center: eucalyptus tree photo by olga Yastremska/Alamy. Right: ficus bonsai photo by coroiu octavian/Alamy.

Pages 263, 268 All photos courtesy of JOMO Studio; jomostudio.com.

Page 264 Left: aloe vera photo by Keith Leighton/Alamy. Center: *Crassula* Candy Cane photo courtesy of The Next Gardener. Right: *Crassula* Ivory Towers photo by l_martinez/Alamy.

Page 265 Left: *Crassula* Moonglow photo by kcuxen/AdobeStock. Center: *Echeveria* photo by 2rogan/AdobeStock. Right: tiger jade photo by Cassidy Tuttle/Succulents and Sunshine.

Page 266 Left: *Oxalis triangularis* photo by Photoimpuls/Shutterstock. Center: sundew photo by Henrik Larsson/AdobeStock. Right: gardenia photo by Zee/Alamy.

Page 267 Left: lavender photo by Irina Fischer/ Alamy. Center: kapa-kapa plant photo by natalean/Shutterstock. Right: orchid photo courtesy of JOMO Studio; jomostudio.com.

Page 269 Left: *Begonia* Spacestar Maia courtesy of Beekenkamp Plants B.V. Center: ZZ 'Raven' photo courtesy of JOMO Studio; jomostudio.com. Right: *Calathea* 'Medallion' photo courtesy of JOMO Studio; jomostudio.com.

Page 271 Top: design by Cara Woodhouse; bottom: photo courtesy of Reform.

Page 272 Top: photo courtesy of L'Objet; bottom: photo by Epitavi/Alamy.

Page 273 Photo by Paige Cleveland for Rule of Three Studio.

Page 275 Top: photo of Channel Swivel Chair courtesy of Cuff Studio; bottom: Parquet Segreit, Ca´ Dona/The Dolomites Collection by ARCA.

Page 276 Photo courtesy of Sam Stewart Studio.

Page 277 Photo courtesy of Ini Archibong.

Page 278 Left: photo of Modern Love paint courtesy of Backdrop; right: photo courtesy of Eric Buterbaugh Flowers, Los Angeles.

Page 279 Top: Opera D'Arte marble courtesy of ABC Stone; bottom: photo by Genevieve Garruppo, featuring custom rug design by Cara Woodhouse/The Rug Company.

Page 280 Top: photo courtesy of Riad Tile; bottom: photo courtesy of Bridgett Cochran and Kelly Porter of Porter Teleo.

Page 286 Photo by Yoshihiro Makino; design by Traci Fleming/House of Honey.

Page 288 Design by Juniper.

A Los Angeles office
designed by House of Honey.

ACKNOWLEDGMENTS

As I reflect on the realization of this book, I can't help but acknowledge that little nine-year-old girl (me!) who envisioned this moment while gazing into a mirror having a conversation with herself, knowing that one day she would have a published book. To her steadfast belief, thank you for never letting go of the dream.

This book wouldn't be possible without the support and love of my incredible husband, Dean, who continuously encourages and inspires me to reach greater heights. You are my guiding light, keeping me grounded and focused.

For my children, Cash and Lennon, your boundless love fuels my determination every single day. Everything I do, I do for you.

To my mother, Barbara, my eternal cheerleader, and to my father, Barry, a shining example of dedication and hard work, your constant support and values have shaped me into who I am today.

Brandi Bowles and the team at United Talent, thank you so much for your belief in my vision and for helping facilitate the opportunity to create my first design book. Emma Mitchell, thank you for finding and believing in this project.

To Laura Dozier, your vision and support have been instrumental in bringing this book to life. A heartfelt thank-you to the entire Abrams publishing team for believing in this project and making my first book experience so exceptional. And cheers to the village of people behind the scenes who kept everything moving: Deb Wood, Hannah Braden, Annalea Manalili, Larry Pekarek, and Jenice Kim.

To Jennifer Wagner, thank you for your brilliant designs. To the stylists, photographers, and visual magic makers, thank you: Joanna McClure, Genevieve Garruppo, Kate Bergeron, Julieanne Browning, and Gabriel Zimmer. All my gratitude to Bodhi Holistic Spa in Hudson, New York, for loaning us so many beautiful crystal specimens to photograph for this book. A special thank-you to Jenny Pouech for procuring and organizing our photography.

Cara Gibbs, your multifaceted brilliance in writing, connecting, and creativity is an immense source of inspiration. Your unique talent and support have been such a contribution to this book. Thank you, from the depths of my heart, for everything.

Daniel Tuttle, you've been my constant companion on this incredible journey. Your many roles as my confidant, coach, and best friend have been vital. You truly are my everything.

And to Heather Summerville, saving the best for last, you've been the foundation and driving force behind this book. Your leadership, dedication, and commitment have shaped this project into reality. You're not only an exceptional writer but also an extraordinary human being whom I'm immensely proud to call a friend. This book could not have gotten done without you!

To each one of you, your contributions and support have made this book possible. I am forever grateful for your presence in my life.

With heartfelt gratitude.